TECHNOLOGICAL INNOVATION HOW INFLUENCES HUMAN

BEHAVIORAL CHANGE

JOHN LOK

Contents

Preface

Introduction

How developed and developing countries technological innovation may influence human behavioral change? How to judge whether the country had been either developed or had been developing ? What factors influence the country development speed? In my this book, I shall indicate New Zealand whether is one developed country or developing country, although its farming industry , e.g. sheep cloth manufacturing, breef and pork meat food export industries had developed long time, but what weaknesses, it owns to influence its continue development easily as well as what strengths it lacks to influence New Zealand is still staying in the developing stage in possible in global leading position. What factors influence US, UK their technological development can not be continued innovated to cause worse development to compare Germany 's heavy manufacturing industry future development in possible. In my this book cuntry development part, I shall concentrate on discussing these above countries' future development trend. Readers can have more clear judgement how they can develop more rapidly. Why do our societies need to innovate? Product innovation, medical technology innovation, space technology innovation, transport service innovation, educational innovation. I shall concentrate on discuss these several aspects. If our societies can not be innovated on above several aspect, then what negative impact may bring to influence our societies. I shall attempt to indicate some evidences to explain what negative impact will cause if our future societies can not innovate to above several aspects in success. I hope my readers can make personal judgement whether my analysis and opinion is right or wrong as well as you can discuss your opinion to argue my view point after you read this book.

In my this book, I shall indicate how our future transportation tool may be invented in order to improve our qualify of lives or standard of lives to be better. How to improve our future transport tools in order to avoid air pollution more serious? It is my this book discussion about how transport invention or improvement, it will influence public transport passenger service and comfortable need aim. I shall attempt to research how transport improvement question in order to let readers feel how it can influence future public transport tools passenger individual choosing any kinds of pubic transport tools need as well as how is our future actual transport improvement achievement aim in order to keep our standard of lives (quality of lives) can be improved to achieve the best service standard and avoid any kinds of future public transport tools passengers number reduces. Because any public transport needs to be improved in order to satisfy passengers comfortable needs. IN passenger comfortable need psychology view, how to improve public transport service quality. It is my main discussion in this book topic, it concerns bus, ferry and rail public transport passenger psychology.

This book final chapter aims to explain how to apply artificial intelligent machine men to teach students in University. If one day, artificial intelligent machine men can be invent to own human's mind and judgement abilities. I believe that universities can attempt to apply artificial intelligent machine men to teach students in lecturer hall. When, artificial intelligent machine men can be invented to learn how to reading any books, writing any books, learning any subject knowledge, even learn how to make judgement to answer any students studying challenges. Then, it is possible that they can be applied to replace universities lecturers their teaching jobs to teach students in univeristy hall.

Prologue

Table of content

which can influence the country's macro consumption desire?
Can technology influence human shopping behavioral change?

Why and how human behavior may influence the country's economic growth or recession?
Technology how impacts human behavior changing?
How and why employees behaviors may influence economy development?
Robots invention whether they can help organizations to raise efficiencies or inefficiencies?
Why social behavior may influence organizational strategy needs to be changed ?
How and why human behavior may influence economic growth or recession? p.161-195

CHAPTER I

Reasons Medical Technology Needs To Be Innovate

Medical technology improvement how brings medical equipment and medical health service performance improvement

Nowadays, our medical technology had been improving, patients can give excellent medical equipment and medical service to raise their health improvement ratio, human's life can be also prolong. Instead of medical technology improvement can help patients to improve health better aspect, whether medical technology can bring other benefits , such as social development, GDP growth, create job chance, improvement hospital service performance to let patients to feel more satisfactory these aspects.

This report is based on a 2018 Healthcare Analytics Summit presentation entitled, "Innovative Analytics: Using Analytics to Evaluate Emerging Technologies."(January 23, 2019).It indicated that "U.S. healthcare spending alone is larger than the gross domestic product of most nations. Total health spending in the U.S. was $3.5 trillion in 2017 and is projected to grow by an average of 5.5 percent annually from 2017 to 2026. If all U.S. healthcare spending was separated into its own sovereign nation, it would constitute the fifth largest economy in the world. Much of those healthcare dollars is spent on the costs of cardiovascular disease, which surpassed both Alzheimer's disease and diabetes with a cost of $318 billion in 2015. That number is projected to more than double to $749 billion in 2035. Additionally, consumers and providers are not experiencing a great return on investment in healthcare dollars. In fact, life expectancy in the U.S. does not compare favorably to other countries which spend less per capita on healthcare.

These skyrocketing costs have a big impact on consumers, with premiums increasing by 74 percent from 2007 to 2017. During that same period, employer contributions increased by an average of 48 percent. The impacts are also being felt by hospitals and providers. In 2016, 30 percent of all Medicare fee-for-service patients were part of alternative payment models; that number rose to 50 percent in 2018. As healthcare systems are squeezed in all directions, they need to determine how to cut costs and still provide high-quality care. To do so, they will need to look across the care continuum for answers, eliminate silos, reduce variation in care, and look to emerging technologies."

Why does medical technology need to be innovate? There are two types of variation in healthcare: necessary and unnecessary. Necessary variation is deviation from standardized care based on individual patient characteristics resulting in improved outcomes. Unnecessary variation does not result in a benefit to the patient and instead increases cost. Variation in practice patterns has been studied in multiple conditions and the conclusion is that higher cost regions are not associated with improved quality or outcomes. While health systems have to look at variation in care in order to reduce unwanted variation, they can look within their own four walls to gain insights from data in order to reduce costs and improve care. So, if medical equipment technology can be innovated, it can bring cost reduces benefit to hospitals as well as patients can get more health benefit and they can also feel more satisfactory and comfortable feeling when they need to live in any one hospital room.

● How to Improve Outcomes and Decrease Costs for hospitals ?

Health systems have struggled to answer the question of how to improve outcomes and decrease costs. New solutions are needed to answer an old problem. Healthcare systems can focus on these four pillars of healthcare improvement, when medical technology can be innovated in success, it can bring these benefits to any hospitals in possible, they may include :

Population Health Management – Improve the health of the population through adherence to clinical guidelines across the continuum. Quantify the population needs and measure adherence to clinical guidelines.

Develop strategies and tools to improve care access and efficiency.

Reduce Clinical Variation – Transform care delivery through the reduction of clinical variation. Reduce unnecessary variation in clinical care.

Standardize care pathways and protocols.

Increase value.

Test New Processes of Care and Payment Models – Transform care delivery by piloting new and creative processes and payment models. Build on existing best practice programs and protocols to improve quality and efficiency in care delivery.

Develop and test new payment models.

Leverage Cutting Emerging Healthcare Technology – Explore new ways to

efficiently care for patients. Implantable monitors.
Complex procedures and surgeries.
As emerging healthcare technology comes into greater focus, it's important for healthcare systems to evaluate the safety and effectiveness in order to effectively harness new technology for better care and reduced costs.
Optimizing Care Across the Cardiovascular Continuum
Additionally, in looking for the highest impact projects to tackle, health systems can look to optimize care across the cardiovascular continuum:
Primary Care – providers can emphasize a healthy lifestyle, use routine treatment protocols, and follow referral protocols.
Outpatient Cardiology – provide timely access to specialists, use guideline driven testing and treatment, and employ comprehensive diagnostic testing.
Sub-Specialty Care and Emergency Services – Standardize emergency care and protocols for complex patients requiring further evaluation and treatment.
Advanced Therapies – Look at whether the right patients are receiving right complex procedures.
Thus, all of above medical expenditure cost reduces and medical service performance improvement may be caused when any hospital begins to attempt to spend some expenditure to get long term medical equipment life useful benefits fot their patients. It is one good behavioral economic benefit to any hospitals.

● Why medical equipment innovation can bring medical improvement ?

Medical innovations can have vastly improved the human condition. Our pharmaceutical, biotech, medical technology, device and diagnostics companies have helped people live longer, with less pain and greater quality of life. Over the past century, the life sciences has eradicated some of the world's most dreaded diseases such as polio and smallpox. More recently, the industry has made other diseases such as breast cancer, HIV/AIDS, heart disease and lung cancer no longer the death sentences that they once were.

What is Medical Innovation's Overlooked Benefit ? With these medical innovations, past and future, comes an often-overlooked benefit: the incalculable billions of dollars in savings to patients, their families, insurers, employers, governments and hospitals in avoided medical expenses associated with keeping people healthy or curing them of a life-long, chronic condition. Certainly, these medicines, therapies, medical technologies, devices and diagnostic tools keep people healthier. They limit the need for frequent visits to the doctor. They help to avoid costly hospital stays. They help patients avoid expensive surgeries. Unfortunately, these tremendous cost savings often go unrecognized. Instead, we hear frequent reports about the high cost of medicine or about new technologies or diagnostic tools being deemed “too expensive” or “unnecessary.” We hear that medical innovation is a cost-driver, not a cost-saver. Thus, when any hospitals‘ medical equipment can be innovated to bring more advaned surgeon equipment or any cancer patient, brain patient user facility. Consequently, in long term, I believe that it can help any hospitals to reduce long time medical equipment repairement expense, in economic benefit, it can help any hospitals to save cost to need to buy any new medical equipment when they are old or bad, if the hospitals can spend some extra expenditure to buy any new innovated medical equipment for their patients to use in long time. It means that spending less expenditure earn long time cost reducing benefit to the hospital, in economic benefit view, it is value to any hospitals to choose " spending less expenditure for medical equipment innovative expenditure.

The reality is quite to the contrary. Medications, therapies and medical technologies and devices not only save lives — they save money. By eradicating a disease, people no longer need to seek or spend money on treatment. By better managing and preventing more serious complications from an existing disease, people avoid more costly medical care. By discovering a new treatment or cure, the costs that would have been incurred in addressing a patient’s ongoing medical issues can be avoided entirely. Therefore, developing new treatments, cures and health technologies is one of the most important steps we can take — not only to save lives and improve the quality of life, but also to avoid the expenditure of enormous amounts of health care dollars.

reference

Analytics and Outcomes Improvement, How to Evaluate Emerging Healthcare Technology With Innovative Analytics , From :https://www.healthcatalyst.com/insights/how-evaluate-emerging-healthcare-technology January 23, 2019

Medical technology improvement brings what social influences

How much savings does medical innovation produce? There is not one, simple answer to that question. However, there are numerous academic and government statistics that point to the economic benefits of innovation in the health-care marketplace. In a paper published by the Journal of Political Economy in 2006, it was estimated that over the preceding 50 years, medical innovation had been the source of nearly half of all economic growth in the United States. Impressively, for every dollar spent on innovative medicines, total healthcare spending is reduced by $7.20, according to an NBER paper. As for the price of medicine in America, only 9 cents of every health care dollar spent in America goes to medicines, according to the Centers for Medicare & Medicaid Services (CMS) in 2013. The other 91 cents goes to hospitals, physicians, clinics, long-term care facilities, and government administration and net cost of health insurance. Imagine if we could use that 9 cents to reduce the remaining 91 cents or even avoid significant portions of it in the first place. The result would be saved lives and even greater health-care savings. So, if medical innovation succeeds, then the country will reduce much medicine expense. It implies that medical innovation can help many people reduce to spend medical expenditure, such as medicine expenditure is reduced because they can have more health. Whewn many people can have more health, our burden for medical expense will also be influenced to reduce. It is one good example of social medical expense reducing, when our medical technology improvement system is innovated in success.

However, healthCare Institute of New Jersey (HINJ) President and Chief Executive Officer Dean J. Paranicas Dec. 18, (2014) has authored the following op-ed on the life sciences and the value of medical innovation, he indicated that medication adherence also plays an important role in health-care savings, as medical innovations can provide no benefit if they are not accessed by patients. Of the approximately 187 million Americans who take one or more prescription drugs, it is estimated that up to one-half do not take their medications as prescribed. Poor medication adherence results in 33 to 69 percent of medication-related hospital admissions in the U.S., at a cost of roughly $100 billion per year. In total, non-adherence to prescribed medicines results in approximately $290 billion in unnecessary spending annually. Americans with chronic conditions account for 84 percent of health care spending. In 2011, this totaled more than $2 trillion. By using medical innovations to prevent or better manage the most common chronic diseases, the U.S. could decrease treatment costs by $218 billion per year and reduce the economic impact of disease by $1.1 trillion annually. For diabetes, the total costs of this chronic disease rose to $245 billion in

2012 from $174 billion in 2007. Without a cure, in the next 25 years, annual spending on diabetes is forecast to increase steeply to approximately $336 billion annually. For Alzheimer's disease, in the absence of disease-modifying treatments, the cumulative costs of care for people suffering with Alzheimer's from 2010 to 2050 are expected to exceed $20 trillion. A treatment breakthrough that only postpones the onset of Alzheimer's by as few as five years could result in annual Medicare savings of $33 billion in 2020 and climb to $283 billion by mid-century, while annual Medicaid savings could increase from $9 billion in 2020 to $79 billion in 2050.

Hence, when US medical innovation succeeds, then it can reduce much diseases occur and medicine cost may be influenced to reduce because ther are not many patients need to buy medicine to eat in US drug market. Consequently, when drug cost reduces, e.g. US drug price is $100 for one kind of diseasem it may be influenced to reduce to $10 in US drug market. Then many US patients do not need to feel drug burden to buy expensive drug to eat when US medical technology can be innovated in success.

reference

New Brunswick, NJ— HealthCare Institute of New Jersey (HINJ) Dean J. Paranicas "the life sciences and the value of medical innovation. " December 18, 2014

https://hinj.org/the-value-of-medical-innovation-saving-lives-saving-money/

Medical technology improvement and GDP growth and job creation relationship

Can medical technology immprovement or medical innovation influence GDP growth? I beleive that medical innovation can help some countries GDP growth significantly. For India example, it is one high population ratio country, it must have many people need to get medical health service when they need to live in any one India hospital. So, India's medical health sector has high GDP income percentage to compare other industries sectors in India. For COVID 19 disease example, it influences many India patients to give this kind of disease to cause they need to live in India hospitals nowadays. So, India must need to innovate its medical equipment or improve its medical equipment or medical health service performance in order to satisfy India COVID 19 disease patients their living hospitals needs in long time, it may be one year, even two years or more for this COVID 19 disease occurs.

Medical innovation is essential for sustainable growth and economic development. Several core conditions enable innovation and encourage economic growth. In the modern economy, innovation is crucial for value creation, growth and employment and innovation processes take place at the enterprise, regional and national level. Innovation will lead to new businesses as well as to the increased competitiveness of existing enterprises. So, the country's any hospitals ' medical innovation will have indirect relatioship to help the country itself economy growth in possible.

Innovations represent a process, namely an activity of creating a new product or service, new technologic process, new organization, or enhancement of existing product or service, existing technologic process and existing organization. According to the given definition, if we analyze its separate elements, we can say that we classify: innovations in production – development or enhancement of a specific product; innovations in services – offering new or enhancing of existing services; innovations in process – finding of new ways of organizing and combining inputs in the process of production of specific products or services; and innovations in management –creating new ways of organizing business resources. So, when one hospital or one country's overall medical system can be innovated in success, it will help the country or society to create a new medical drug or medical service improvement, new medical technologic innovative process, new hospital organizational medical service culture changing or enhancement of existing medical service performance or medical drug product manufacturing improvement to bring positive new medical innovation to impact the country's economy.

In economic benefit view, when the country has many hospitals feel need to change new medical equipment to replace their old medical equipment. Then, due to there are many hospital medical equipment buyers number increases or their medical equipment need number increases, then it will influence the country will have many medical equipment manufactures hope to manufacture different kinds of medical equipment to sell to themselves country's hospital organization buyers. So, it will influence the country's medical equipment market grows up. Consequently, this country's medical sector GDP growth ratio will be influenced to raise significantly. SO, such as India medical equipment market case, if COVID 19 disease still attacks to India itself country to cause many people feel disease. Then, it will influence many Indian need to live hospitals. Consequently, India will have many hospitals will need to buy many medical equipment to prepare for these Indian patients when they are contacting COVID 19 disease. In long term, India's medical equipment manufacturers ought need to prepare to increase medical equipment number to supply to India patients need when they are contracting COVID 19 disease. Finally, India's medical equipment demand number and supply number will begin to increase. It will create medical equipment job chance and any medical equipment manufacturers income will be influenced to increase when there are many India hospitals need to buy many medical equipment to prepare to supply to India COVID 19 disease patients to use in long time.

Wh Is The Innovation Economy?

To fully understand what the innovation economy is, it is important to first know how it came about. The theory of this form of economics was developed only in the last few decades. Previously, the growth of the economy was det

Is medical technology improvement essential to our future medical social service ?

Finally, I shall ask our societies whether we must need to improve our nowadays medical technology to be better in order to raise medical service performance improvement to satisfy global patients medical service care needs. To answer this question. We need to consider why our medical technology needs to be improve and what will be worse if future our global medical technology can not be improved in success.

I shall indicate COVID 19 disease occurrence case example, it is one good example to explain why our global medical societies need to be improved immediately. Nowadays, there are many health people become patients, even they die easily due to they do not know where they go out to contact this COVID 19 patients in indoor or outdoor natural environment factor. In fact, global COVID disease patients number is continue increasing. There are many COVID 19 disease patients need to live hospitals. If they can not get enough medical equipment when they are living in hospitals, then they can not prolong lives easily. Such as India and Afica , they are developing countries, when COVID 19 disease had been coming to these both countries to cause many Indian and Afican get this COVID 19 disease to be die easily. In fact, these both coutries have many people are killed by COVID 19 disease. Even, developed countries, e.g. US , UK , there are many health people are killed by COVID disease.

I have no interest to discuss whether why and how COVID 19 disease can kill any health people to any countries. I have only interest to disease

whether our global societies need to innovate our medical technology in order to save many health people lives. Nowadays, we facing COVID19 disease occurrence, it can cause many health people, old or young age people to die easily. In the future, we do not know whether there are another new kind of disease will come , even more than one new kind of disease will come. So, if we can not find new medical technological method to solve our nowadays old medical technology to be improved, then we will feel difficulty to solve future possible new disease occurs in possible.
ON conclusion, our global medical technological leaders need to sit down together to discuss how to improve our traditional old medical technology to be the best in order to attack future any unknown or new kinds of diseases occur in future any one day. If we do not have enough medical technology to prepare to attack any new kinds of diseases come , then we will have many health people to be killed by any one kind of serious diseases easily. So, it seems that medical technology improvement is essential because we need medical technology improvement to save our lives before any one kind of new disease comes to our societies. If it is too late to innovate our medical technology, then we may have many health people to become patients to be killed by any one kind of new disease in possible.

Technology hasTeTechnology has also made it possible for physicians and care managers to communicate with patients between doctor visits and after hospital discharge. For instance, some apps send automated reminders that ask patients to answer questions after surgery or during healing, and algorithm-dr

Knowledge innovation how brings economic growth
What does knowledge innovation mean? Why and how do we need to continue to innovate our knowledge? Can knowledge innovation impact positive economic growth to our societies? In fact, when we can prepare to innovate our knowledge to be perfect. Consequently, it can help our social development more success, e.g. non manual driving vehicle, e-commerce, construction houses on water skill, hospital new robocit surgeon equipment, manufacturing robotic technology , even space touriusm leisure development etc. different kinds of technology innovation, they are depended on how human can attempt to learn to innovate or improve ourselves traditional old knowledge to be changed to any kinds of new or not discovered unique knowledge. So, human ought need to continue to

learn how to innovate our old traditional knowledger to be more perfect. The question concerns how human can continue to change our old knowledge to innovate in succeed. I shall attempt to indicate factors to answer this question as below:

What does knowledge innovation mean? The role of knowledge innovation means that knowledge management assists in building competencies required in the innovation process. Though knowledge accessibility and knowledge flow to organization, staff memebers are able to increase their skills levels and knowledge both formally and informally. An increase in skills can improve the quality of innovation as well as in society. When the country have many people can attempt to learn how to change and knowledge old knowledge to new knowledge, then they my bring their societies to develop more rapidly. So, it seems that knowledge innovation may help society, organization and individual to bring new knowledge to attribute to our future societies easily. It wil be a very important factor influence human future development in success.

However, knowlege innovation concept is not just represented by introducing or implementing new ideas or methods. The definition of meaning of innovation can be defined as a process, but involves multiple activities to uncover new ways to do things. Innovating helps developing original concepts and is to driver of optimizing operations. The purpose of innovation is to come up with new ideas and technologies that increase productivity and generate greater output with the same input on organizational aspect.

So, knowledge innovation may be applied on organization aspect, even individual and social aspects. On organizational knowledge innovation aspect, innovation secures tomorrow's revenue, lowers costs and differentiates companies from the market. However, a good business model that only provides a brief market advantage and disappears after a year is not the right approach. Hence, organizational knowledge innovation aims to help the organization to raise competitive effort in long term.

Does knowledge provide innovation in organizations? Knowledge managment creates a culture conductive to tacit knowledge creation, sharing ideas in the organization, which plays an important role in the innovation process. Is knowledge management ncecessary for innovation? Beside the financial basis knowledge is the most important resource for innovations, in order to lead a company successfully, systematic handling of " knowledge", becomes more important. Today, the increase in value

develops from the productivity and the innovation in business society.
What is the role of knowledge for individual? Knowledge is important for personal growth and development, knowledge sharpens our skills like reasoning and problem solving. A strong base of knowledge helps brains function more smoothly and effectively. We become smarter with the power of knowledge and solve problems more easily. Hence, innovation is about knowledge creating new possibilities through combining different knowledge sets. These can be in the form of knowledge about what is technically possible or not particular configuration of this world meet an articulated or latent need.
For knowledge innovation can bring the positive effects of technology improvement example, there are just a few of the ways in which technology may positively affect our physical and mental health. Health apps to track chronic ilnesses and communicate vitual information to doctors , health apps that anyone tracks diet, any kinds of sport exercise and mental health information . Hence, technololgy innovation had been applied to health apps smart phone product to help we to track our health from ourselves smart phone apps equipment easily any time.
What impact did this innovation have on daily life? It increased the regional differences among various groups of people across the country, it become a major method of long distance commnication to many years. It allowed people to sign documents from across the country. So, innovation can be applied to administive tasks aspect. Also, it can increase productivity and brings citizens new and better goods and services that improves our overall standard of living.
The benefits of inovation are sometimes slow to materialize. They often fell broadly across the entire population. According to Krathwohl (2002), he indicated that knowledge can be categorized into four types: (1) factual knowledge (2) conceptual knowledge (3) procedural knowledge and (4) metacognitive knowledge. So, if human hopes to implement knowledge innovation in success, we need to know how to learn these 4 types of knowledge innovation elements. For organizational knowledge management components example, the best four components are people, process, content/ IT and strategy.
Regardless of the industry size or knowledge needs of your organizations, organizations always need people to lead, sponsor, and support knowledge sharing. Sharing knowledge innovation how influences social development. Social innovation includes social processes of innovation, such as open

source methods and techniques and also the innovation which have a social purpose, like activism , virtual volunteering, or distance learning. Social innovation may include the social processes of innovation. However, social innovation is important because it can provide a unique opportunity to step back from a narrow way of thinking about social enterprise, business engagement and to recognize instead the interconnectedness of various factors and stakeholders. For science and technolgical social innovation example, science and technology can help a nation's process and development science and technology innovation are connected with development because they have hostorical record of bringing advances that have led to healthier, longer, weathler and more productive lives and they are key ingredients to solutions to the most serious poverty and economic development challenges.

So, social innovation may bring human benefits, such as providing food and lifestyle products world wide with focus on environmental and social innovation , giveing every child in the world the chance to learn code and helping the visually impaired interact with their surroundings. Hence, social innovation means new solutions (products, services, models, markets, processes etc.) that stimultaneously meet a social need (more effectively than existing solutions) and lead to new or improved capabilities and relationships and better use of assets and resources. However, a social innovation process consists of a sequence of activities that seals to find solutions to a special challenge. The process itself brings a new approach that has social impact in its means (process) and ends (solution).

There are 6 keys characteristics of a social innovation, as told by Colombian social enterprises, they include: Adresses real needs of people in a community, requires a deep understanding of the problem, localizes and humanizes the problem, builds trust and collaborates with the community in need, is sustainable and scalable and adapts constantly. Hence, every one may attempt to learn in social innovation. You will learn what social innovations are and understand how they are help solve societal problems. You will get an overview of important literature and debates on social innovation. You will also learn and apply methods to develop , implement and scale social innovations.

How can social innovation be improved? Major cross business/cross functional projects should also have social innovation objectives include: leadership programs that include volunteering activities may help employees develop their skills and lead to greater innovations during their daily work in any organizations. How does the idea of social innovation connect with social needs? We define social innovations as new approaches to addressing social needs. They are social in their means and in their ends. They engage and mobilize the beneficiaries and help the transform social relations by improving beneficiaries' access to power and resources.

For social innovation on education aspect, teaching technological literacy, critical thinking and problem, solving through science education gives students the skills and knowledge, they need to succeed in school and beyond. The essence of how science and technology contributes to society in the creation of new knowledge , and then utilization of that knowledge to boost the prosperity of human lives, and to solve the various issues facing society.

On conclusion, social innovation may be future social knowledge innovation to help us to solve problems, it is an issue within the society that makes it difficult for people to achieve their full potential issue, e.g. poverty, unemployment, unequal opportunity, racism and mainutrition are examples of social problems , even housing shortagfe, employment discrimination and child abuse and neglect. Thus, as above evidences indication, they can explain why we must need to innovate our future knowledge in order to help us to solve any organizations, social and individuals challenges more easily.

Medical technology improvement how brings medical equipment and medical health service performance improvement

Nowadays, our medical technology had been improving, patients can give excellent medical equipment and medical service to raise their health improvement ratio, human's life can be also prolong. Instead of medical technology improvement can help patients to improve health better aspect, whether medical technology can bring other benefits , such as social development, GDP growth, create job chance, improvement hospital service performance to let patients to feel more satisfactory these aspects.

This report is based on a 2018 Healthcare Analytics Summit presentation entitled, "Innovative Analytics: Using Analytics to Evaluate Emerging Technologies."(January 23, 2019).It indicated that "U.S. healthcare spending alone is larger than the gross domestic product of most nations. Total health spending in the U.S. was $3.5 trillion in 2017 and is projected to grow by an average of 5.5 percent annually from 2017 to 2026. If all U.S. healthcare spending was separated into its own sovereign nation, it would constitute the fifth largest economy in the world. Much of those healthcare dollars is spent on the costs of cardiovascular disease, which surpassed both Alzheimer's disease and diabetes with a cost of $318 billion in 2015. That number is projected to more than double to $749 billion in 2035. Additionally, consumers and providers are not experiencing a great return on investment in healthcare dollars. In fact, life expectancy in the U.S. does not compare favorably to other countries which spend less per capita on healthcare.

These skyrocketing costs have a big impact on consumers, with premiums increasing by 74 percent from 2007 to 2017. During that same period, employer contributions increased by an average of 48 percent. The impacts are also being felt by hospitals and providers. In 2016, 30 percent of all Medicare fee-for-service patients were part of alternative payment models; that number rose to 50 percent in 2018. As healthcare systems are squeezed in all directions, they need to determine how to cut costs and still provide high-quality care. To do so, they will need to look across the care continuum for answers, eliminate silos, reduce variation in care, and look to emerging technologies."

Why does medical technology need to be innovate? There are two types of variation in healthcare: necessary and unnecessary. Necessary variation is deviation from standardized care based on individual patient characteristics resulting in improved outcomes. Unnecessary variation does not result in a benefit to the patient and instead increases cost. Variation in practice patterns has been studied in multiple conditions and the conclusion is that higher cost regions are not associated with improved quality or outcomes. While health systems have to look at variation in care in order to reduce unwanted variation, they can look within their own four walls to gain insights from data in order to reduce costs and improve care. So, if medical equipment technology can be innovated, it can bring cost reduces benefit to hospitals as well as patients can get more health benefit and they can also feel more satisfactory and comfortable feeling when they need to live in any one hospital room.

● How to Improve Outcomes and Decrease Costs for hospitals ?

Health systems have struggled to answer the question of how to improve outcomes and decrease costs. New solutions are needed to answer an old problem. Healthcare systems can focus on these four pillars of healthcare improvement, when medical technology can be innovated in success, it can bring these benefits to any hospitals in possible, they may include :

Population Health Management – Improve the health of the population through adherence to clinical guidelines across the continuum. Quantify the population needs and measure adherence to clinical guidelines.
Develop strategies and tools to improve care access and efficiency.
Reduce Clinical Variation – Transform care delivery through the reduction of clinical variation. Reduce unnecessary variation in clinical care.
Standardize care pathways and protocols.
Increase value.
Test New Processes of Care and Payment Models – Transform care delivery by piloting new and creative processes and payment models. Build on existing best practice programs and protocols to improve quality and efficiency in care delivery.
Develop and test new payment models.
Leverage Cutting Emerging Healthcare Technology – Explore new ways to efficiently care for patients. Implantable monitors.
Complex procedures and surgeries.
As emerging healthcare technology comes into greater focus, it's important for healthcare systems to evaluate the safety and effectiveness in order to effectively harness new technology for better care and reduced costs.
Optimizing Care Across the Cardiovascular Continuum
Additionally, in looking for the highest impact projects to tackle, health systems can look to optimize care across the cardiovascular continuum:
Primary Care – providers can emphasize a healthy lifestyle, use routine treatment protocols, and follow referral protocols.
Outpatient Cardiology – provide timely access to specialists, use guideline driven testing and treatment, and employ comprehensive diagnostic testing.
Sub-Specialty Care and Emergency Services – Standardize emergency care and protocols for complex patients requiring further evaluation and treatment.
Advanced Therapies – Look at whether the right patients are receiving right complex procedures.
Thus, all of above medical expenditure cost reduces and medical service performance improvement may be caused when any hospital begins to attempt to spend some expenditure to get long term medical equipment life useful benefits fot their patients. It is one good behavioral economic benefit to any hospitals.

● Why medical equipment innovation can bring medical improvement ?

Medical innovations can have vastly improved the human condition. Our pharmaceutical, biotech, medical technology, device and diagnostics companies have helped people live longer, with less pain and greater quality of life. Over the past century, the life sciences has eradicated some of the world's most dreaded diseases such as polio and smallpox. More recently, the industry has made other diseases such as breast cancer, HIV/AIDS, heart disease and lung cancer no longer the death sentences that they once were.

What is Medical Innovation's Overlooked Benefit ? With these medical innovations, past and future, comes an often-overlooked benefit: the incalculable billions of dollars in savings to patients, their families, insurers, employers, governments and hospitals in avoided medical expenses associated with keeping people healthy or curing them of a life-long, chronic condition. Certainly, these medicines, therapies, medical technologies, devices and diagnostic tools keep people healthier. They limit the need for frequent visits to the doctor. They help to avoid costly hospital stays. They help patients avoid expensive surgeries. Unfortunately, these tremendous cost savings often go unrecognized. Instead, we hear frequent reports about the high cost of medicine or about new technologies or diagnostic tools being deemed "too expensive" or "unnecessary." We hear that medical innovation is a cost-driver, not a cost-saver. Thus, when any hospitals' medical equipment can be innovated to bring more advaned surgeon equipment or any cancer patient, brain patient user facility. Consequently, in long term, I believe that it can help any hospitals to reduce long time medical equipment repairement expense, in economic benefit, it can help any hospitals to save cost to need to buy any new medical equipment when they are old or bad, if the hospitals can spend some extra expenditure to buy any new innovated medical equipment for their patients to use in long time. It means that spending less expenditure earn long time cost reducing benefit to the hospital, in economic benefit view, it is value to any hospitals to choose " spending less expenditure for medical equipment innovative expenditure.

The reality is quite to the contrary. Medications, therapies and medical technologies and devices not only save lives — they save money. By eradicating a disease, people no longer need to seek or spend money on treatment. By better managing and preventing more serious complications from an existing disease, people avoid more costly medical care. By discovering a new treatment or cure, the costs that would have been incurred in addressing a patient's ongoing medical issues can be avoided entirely. Therefore, developing new treatments, cures and health technologies is one of the most important steps we can take — not only to save lives and improve the quality of life, but also to avoid the expenditure of enormous amounts of health care dollars.

reference
Analytics and Outcomes Improvement, How to Evaluate Emerging Healthcare Technology With Innovative Analytics , From :https://www.healthcatalyst.com/insights/how-evaluate-emerging-healthcare-technology January 23, 2019

Medical technology improvement brings what social influences
How much savings does medical innovation produce? There is not one, simple answer to that question. However, there are numerous academic and government statistics that point to the economic benefits of innovation in the health-care marketplace. In a paper published by the Journal of Political Economy in 2006, it was estimated that over the preceding 50 years, medical innovation had been the source of nearly half of all economic growth in the United States. Impressively, for every dollar spent on innovative medicines, total healthcare spending is reduced by $7.20, according to an NBER paper. As for the price of medicine in America, only 9 cents of every health care dollar spent in America goes to medicines, according to the Centers for Medicare & Medicaid Services (CMS) in 2013. The other 91 cents goes to hospitals, physicians, clinics, long-term care facilities, and government administration and net cost of health insurance. Imagine if we could use that 9 cents to reduce the remaining 91 cents or even avoid significant portions of it in the first place. The result would be saved lives and even greater health-care savings. So, if medical innovation succeeds, then the country will reduce much medicine expense. It implies that medical innovation can help many people reduce to spend medical expenditure, such as medicine expenditure is reduced because they can have more health. Whewn many people can have more health, our burden for medical expense will also be influenced to reduce. It is one good example of social medical expense reducing, when our medical technology improvement system is innovated in success.
However, healthCare Institute of New Jersey (HINJ) President and Chief Executive Officer Dean J. Paranicas Dec. 18, (2014) has authored the following op-ed on the life sciences and the value of medical innovation, he

indicated that medication adherence also plays an important role in health-care savings, as medical innovations can provide no benefit if they are not accessed by patients. Of the approximately 187 million Americans who take one or more prescription drugs, it is estimated that up to one-half do not take their medications as prescribed. Poor medication adherence results in 33 to 69 percent of medication-related hospital admissions in the U.S., at a cost of roughly $100 billion per year. In total, non-adherence to prescribed medicines results in approximately $290 billion in unnecessary spending annually. Americans with chronic conditions account for 84 percent of health care spending. In 2011, this totaled more than $2 trillion. By using medical innovations to prevent or better manage the most common chronic diseases, the U.S. could decrease treatment costs by $218 billion per year and reduce the economic impact of disease by $1.1 trillion annually. For diabetes, the total costs of this chronic disease rose to $245 billion in 2012 from $174 billion in 2007. Without a cure, in the next 25 years, annual spending on diabetes is forecast to increase steeply to approximately $336 billion annually. For Alzheimer's disease, in the absence of disease-modifying treatments, the cumulative costs of care for people suffering with Alzheimer's from 2010 to 2050 are expected to exceed $20 trillion. A treatment breakthrough that only postpones the onset of Alzheimer's by as few as five years could result in annual Medicare savings of $33 billion in 2020 and climb to $283 billion by mid-century, while annual Medicaid savings could increase from $9 billion in 2020 to $79 billion in 2050.
Hence, when US medical innovation succeeds, then it can reduce much diseases occur and medicine cost may be influenced to reduce because ther are not many patients need to buy medicine to eat in US drug market. Consequently, when drug cost reduces, e.g. US drug price is $100 for one kind of diseasem it may be influenced to reduce to $10 in US drug market. Then many US patients do not need to feel drug burden to buy expensive drug to eat when US medical technology can be innovated in success.

reference

New Brunswick, NJ— HealthCare Institute of New Jersey (HINJ) Dean J. Paranicas "the life sciences and the value of medical innovation. " December 18, 2014
https://hinj.org/the-value-of-medical-innovation-saving-lives-saving-money/

Medical technology improvement and GDP growth and job creation relationship
Can medical technology immprovement or medical innovation influence GDP growth? I beleive that medical innovation can help some countries GDP growth significantly. For India example, it is one high population ratio country, it must have many people need to get medical health service when they need to live in any one India hospital. So, India's medical health sector has high GDP income percentage to compare other industries sectors in India. For COVID 19 disease example, it influences many India patients to give this kind of disease to cause they need to live in India hospitals nowadays. So, India must need to innovate its medical equipment or improve its medical equipment or medical health service performance in order to satisfy India COVID 19 disease patients their living hospitals needs in long time, it may be one year, even two years or more for this COVID 19 disease occurs.
Medical innovation is essential for sustainable growth and economic development. Several core conditions enable innovation and encourage economic growth. In the modern economy, innovation is crucial for value creation, growth and employment and innovation processes take
place at the enterprise, regional and national level. Innovation will lead to new businesses as well as to the increased competitiveness of existing enterprises. So, the country's any hospitals ' medical innovation will have indirect relatioship to help the country itself economy growth in possible.

Innovations represent a process, namely an activity of creating a
new product or service, new technologic process, new organization, or
enhancement of existing product or service, existing technologic process
and existing organization. According to the given definition, if we analyze its separate elements, we can say that we classify: innovations in production – development or enhancement of a specific product; innovations in services – offering new or enhancing of existing services; innovations in process – finding of new ways of organizing and combining inputs in the
process of production of specific products or services; and innovations in management –creating new ways of organizing business resources. So, when one hospital or one country's overall medical system can be innovated in success, it will help the country or society to create a new medical drug or medical service improvement, new medical technologic innovative process, new hospital organizational medical service culture changing or enhancement of existing medical service performance or medical drug

product manufacturing improvement to bring positive new medical innovation to impact the country's economy.

In economic benefit view, when the country has many hospitals feel need to change new medical equipment to replace their old medical equipment. Then, due to there are many hospital medical equipment buyers number increases or their medical equipment need number increases, then it will influence the country will have many medical equipment manufactures hope to manufacture different kinds of medical equipment to sell to themselves country's hospital organization buyers. So, it will influence the country's medical equipment market grows up. Consequently, this country's medical sector GDP growth ratio will be influenced to raise significantly. SO, such as India medical equipment market case, if COVID 19 disease still attacks to India itself country to cause many people feel disease. Then, it will influence many Indian need to live hospitals. Consequently, India will have many hospitals will need to buy many medical equipment to prepare for these Indian patients when they are contacting COVID 19 disease. In long term, India's medical equipment manufacturers ought need to prepare to increase medical equipment number to supply to India patients need when they are contracting COVID 19 disease. Finally, India's medical equipment demand number and supply number will begin to increase. It will create medical equipment job chance and any medical equipment manufacturers income will be influenced to increase when there are many India hospitals need to buy many medical equipment to prepare to supply to India COVID 19 disease patients to use in long time.

Wh Is The Innovation Economy?

To fully understand what the innovation economy is, it is important to first know how it came about. The theory of this form of economics was developed only in the last few decades. Previously, the growth of the economy was det

Is medical technology improvement essential to our future medical social service ?

Finally, I shall ask our societies whether we must need to improve our nowadays medical technology to be better in order to raise medical service performance improvement to satisfy global patients medical service care needs. To answer this question. We need to consider why our medical technology needs to be improve and what will be worse if future our global medical technology can not be improved in success.

I shall indicate COVID 19 disease occurrence case example, it is one good example to explain why our global medical societies need to be improved immediately. Nowadays, there are many health people become patients, even they die easily due to they do not know where they go out to contact this COVID 19 patients in indoor or outdoor natural environment factor. In fact, global COVID disease patients number is continue increasing. There are many COVID 19 disease patients need to live hospitals. If they can not get enough medical equipment when they are living in hospitals, then they can not prolong lives easily. Such as India and Afica , they are developing countries, when COVID 19 disease had been coming to these both countries to cause many Indian and Afican get this COVID 19 disease to be die easily. In fact, these both coutries have many people are killed by COVID 19 disease. Even, developed countries, e.g. US , UK , there are many health people are killed by COVID disease.

I have no interest to discuss whether why and how COVID 19 disease can kill any health people to any countries. I have only interest to disease whether our global societies need to innovate our medical technology in order to save many health people lives. Nowadays, we facing COVID19 disease occurrence, it can cause many health people, old or young age people to die easily. In the future, we do not know whether there are another new kind of disease will come , even more than one new kind of disease will come. So, if we can not find new medical technological method to solve our nowadays old medical technology to be improved, then we will feel difficulty to solve future possible new disease occurs in possible.

ON conclusion, our global medical technological leaders need to sit down together to discuss how to improve our traditional old medical technology to be the best in order to attack future any unknown or new kinds of diseases occur in future any one day. If we do not have enough medical technology to prepare to attack any new kinds of diseases come , then we will have many health people to be killed by any one kind of serious diseases easily. So, it seems that medical technology improvement is essential because we need medical technology improvement to save our lives before any one kind of new disease comes to our societies. If it is too late to innovate our medical technology, then we may have many health people to become patients to be killed by any one kind of new disease in possible.

CHAPTER II

Knowledge innovation how brings economic growth

What does knowledge innovation mean? Why and how do we need to continue to innovate our knowledge? Can knowledge innovation impact positive economic growth to our societies? In fact, when we can prepare to innovate our knowledge to be perfect. Consequently, it can help our social development more success, e.g. non manual driving vehicle, e-commerce, construction houses on water skill, hospital new robocit surgeon equipment, manufacturing robotic technology , even space touriusm leisure development etc. different kinds of technology innovation, they are depended on how human can attempt to learn to innovate or improve ourselves traditional old knowledge to be changed to any kinds of new or not discovered unique knowledge. So, human ought need to continue to learn how to innovate our old traditional knowledger to be more perfect. The question concerns how human can continue to change our old knowledge to innovate in succeed. I shall attempt to indicate factors to answer this question as below:

What does knowledge innovation mean? The role of knowledge innovation means that knowledge management assists in building competencies required in the innovation process. Though knowledge accessibility and knowledge flow to organization, staff memebers are able to increase their skills levels and knowledge both formally and informally. An increase in skills can improve the quality of innovation as well as in society. When the country have many people can attempt to learn how to change and knowledge old knowledge to new knowledge, then they my bring their societies to develop more rapidly. So, it seems that knowledge innovation may help society, organization and individual to bring new knowledge to attribute to our future societies easily. It wil be a very important factor influence human future development in success.

However, knowlege innovation concept is not just represented by introducing or implementing new ideas or methods. The definition of meaning of innovation can be defined as a process, but involves multiple activities to uncover new ways to do things. Innovating helps developing original concepts and is to driver of optimizing operations. The purpose of innovation is to come up with new ideas and technologies that increase productivity and generate greater output with the same input on organizational aspect.

So, knowledge innovation may be applied on organization aspect, even individual and social aspects. On organizational knowledge innovation aspect, innovation secures tomorrow's revenue, lowers costs and differentiates companies from the market. However, a good business model that only provides a brief market advantage and disappears after a year is not the right approach. Hence, organizational knowledge innovation aims to help the organization to raise competitive effort in long term.

Does knowledge provide innovation in organizations? Knowledge managment creates a culture conductive to tacit knowledge creation, sharing ideas in the organization, which plays an important role in the innovation process. Is knowledge management ncecessary for innovation? Beside the financial basis knowledge is the most important resource for innovations, in order to lead a company successfully, systematic handling of " knowledge", becomes more important. Today, the increase in value develops from the productivity and the innovation in business society.

What is the role of knowledge for individual? Knowledge is important for personal growth and development, knowledge sharpens our skills like reasoning and problem solving. A strong base of knowledge helps brains function more smoothly and effectively. We become smarter with the power of knowledge and solve problems more easily. Hence, innovation is about knowledge creating new possibilities through combining different knowledge sets. These can be in the form of knowledge about what is technically possible or not particular configuration of this world meet an articulated or latent need.

For knowledge innovation can bring the positive effects of technology improvement example, there are just a few of the ways in which technology may positively affect our physical and mental health. Health apps to track chronic ilnesses and communicate vitual information to doctors , health apps that anyone tracks diet, any kinds of sport exercise and mental health information . Hence, technololgy innovation had been applied to health apps smart phone product to help we to track our health from ourselves smart phone apps equipment easily any time.

What impact did this innovation have on daily life? It increased the regional differences among various groups of people across the country, it become a major method of long distance commnication to many years. It allowed people to sign documents from across the country. So, innovation can be applied to administive tasks aspect. Also, it can increase productivity and brings citizens new and better goods and services that improves our overall standard of living.

The benefits of inovation are sometimes slow to materialize. They often fell broadly across the entire population. According to Krathwohl (2002), he indicated that knowledge can be categorized into four types: (1) factual knowledge (2) conceptual knowledge (3) procedural knowledge and (4) metacognitive knowledge. So, if human hopes to implement knowledge innovation in success, we need to know how to learn these 4 types of knowledge innovation elements. For organizational knowledge management components example, the best four components are people, process, content/ IT and strategy.

Regardless of the industry size or knowledge needs of your organizations, organizations always need people to lead, sponsor, and support knowledge sharing. Sharing knowledge innovation how influences social development. Social innovation includes social processes of innovation, such as open source methods and techniques and also the innovation which have a social purpose, like activism , virtual volunteering, or distance learning. Social innovation may include the social processes of innovation. However, social innovation is important because it can provide a unique opportunity to step back from a narrow way of thinking about social enterprise, business engagement and to recognize instead the interconnectedness of various factors and stakeholders. For science and technolgical social innovation example, science and technology can help a nation's process and development science and technology innovation are connected with development because they have hostorical record of bringing advances that have led to healthier, longer, weathler and more productive lives and they are key ingredients to solutions to the most serious poverty and economic development challenges.

So, social innovation may bring human benefits, such as providing food and lifestyle products world wide with focus on environmental and social innovation , giveing every child in the world the chance to learn code and helping the visually impaired interact with their surroundings. Hence, social innovation means new solutions (products, services, models, markets, processes etc.) that stimultaneously meet a social need (more effectively than existing solutions) and lead to new or improved capabilities and relationships and better use of assets and resources. However, a social innovation process consists of a sequence of activities that seals to find solutions to a special challenge. The process itself brings a new approach that has social impact in its means (process) and ends (solution).

There are 6 keys characteristics of a social innovation, as told by Colombian social enterprises, they include: Adresses real needs of people in a community, requires a deep understanding of the problem, localizes and humanizes the problem, builds trust and collaborates with the community in need, is sustainable and scalable and adapts constantly. Hence, every one may attempt to learn in social innovation. You will learn what social innovations are and understand how they are help solve societal problems. You will get an overview of important literature and debates on social innovation. You will also learn and apply methods to develop , implement and scale social innovations.

How can social innovation be improved? Major cross business/cross functional projects should also have social innovation objectives include: leadership programs that include volunteering activities may help employees develop their skills and lead to greater innovations during their daily work in any organizations. How does the idea of social innovation connect with social needs? We define social innovations as new approaches to addressing social needs. They are social in their means and in their ends. They engage and mobilize the beneficiaries and help the transform social relations by improving beneficiaries' access to power and resources.

For social innovation on education aspect, teaching technological literacy, critical thinking and problem, solving through science education gives students the skills and knowledge, they need to succeed in school and beyond. The essence of how science and technology contributes to society in the creation of new knowledge , and then utilization of that knowledge to boost the prosperity of human lives, and to solve the various issues facing society.

On conclusion, social innovation may be future social knowledge innovation to help us to solve problems, it is an issue within the society that makes it difficult for people to achieve their full potential issue, e.g. poverty, unemployment, unequal opportunity, racism and mainutrition are examples of social problems , even housing shortagfe, employment discrimination and child abuse and neglect. Thus, as above evidences indication, they can explain why we must need to innovate our future knowledge in order to help us to solve any organizations, social and individuals challenges more easily.

CHAPTER III

Organization product and manufacturing process and workplace innovation

Why do businesses need to innovate their products to raise good quality, good design shape to attract custoimers consideration sometimes? What advantages will be bought to the businessmen after their products had been innovated in success? Can products innovation help the product to improve its market image? Can product innovation raise economy growth? I shall attempt to indicate reasons to explain above questions?

In our business societies, any products ought need to be concerned how to innovate them to be good quality. The key practical benefits of innovation may include: Improved productivity, reduced cots, increased competitivenesss, improveed brand recognition and value, building new business partners relationship, helping the business to increase turnover and improved profitability.

So, it seems that product innovation may bring positive impact more than negative impact to any businesses. In fact, after the buysiness innovates itself products, innovation ought may help the business to charge higher prices for new products before competitors products come on the market. Being innovative good for the firm's reputation, even people naturally interested in its future products, if they have been first in the past as well as innovations in processes can add value to existing products/ services.

So, the meant is by product innovation, it means that a product innovation is the introduction of a good or service that is new or significantly improved with respect to its characteristics of intended uses. Maninly, these reasons can explain why innovation is important: Innovation grows business, increasing profit, innovation helps any businesses stay ahead of the competitiion, innovation helps businesses take advantage of new technologies.

On organizational benefit aspect from innovation, innovation may help organizations differentiate themselves , e.g. if your organization is using innovation on its processes, its because doing so will save your time, money, or other resources, and give your organization a competitive advantage over other companies stuck in their system.

In common, innovation may include four types. Incremental, disruptive , archihectural and radical, they help illustrate the various ways that companies can innovate. For technological innovative advantages, it increases productivity and brings citizens new and better goods and services that improve their goods and service that improve their overall standard of living.

The benefits of innovation are sometimes slow to materialize. They often broadly across the entire population. Hence, the advantage of product innovation may include: Growth, expansion and gaining a competitive advantage. A business that is capable of differentiating their product from other businesses in the same industry to large extent will be able to reap profit. Examples of product innovation in improved products involves introducing beter or more functionality to existing products, e.g. electric and gas lawn mower, GPs in car , battery car, non-manual driving auto car etc. So, product innovation is the creation, development and implementation, a new product, process and service, with the aim of improving efficiency, effectiveness or competitive advantages.

How does innovation help the economy? In fact, one of the major benefits of innovation is its contribution to economic growth. Simply put, innovation can lead to higher productivity, meaning that the same input generates a greater output. As productivity rises, more goods and services are producted. In other words, the economy grows.

Instead of innovation on product aspect, innovation is also important in the workplace, it can help staffs to raise efficiency. Innovation is vital in the workplace, because it gives companies an edge in penetrating markets faster and provides a better connection to developing markets, which can lead to bigger opportunities, especially in rich countries or developed countries.

However, when an organization decides to implement innovation before it implements , it needs to concern these possible risks of innovation. Operational risk, e.g. failing to meet your quality, cost or scheduling requirements, commercial risk, e.g. failing to attract enough customers, financial risk,, e.g. investing in unsuccessful innovation projects. But, when the organization decides to implement any innovation, it may hope innovation how contribute to success. Especially as customers become more demanding. Entrepreneurs need an innovation to survive to boost your business productivity, growth and profitability more easily.

IN simple, innovation may improve sales and customer relationship, reduce waste and costs boost your market position, improve employee relations.

What does the right time to organizations make decisions to innovate ? When the firm discovers its customers use the product and they field praise and complaints. And they probably have ideas, however, that can be refined into a better product. Innovative companies make it clear they want ideas, that the door is open and there is always a friendly ear for changes, then they will start to come it. It may be right innovation time, when customers have any unique idea to concern the product after they use.

What is required to introduce innovation in an organization? To successfully implement innovation, you need to know exactly what makes an innovative organization as well as how it contributes to its growth. Our organizaitons also need to require an innovative culture where everyone is able to think independently . So, these reasons can explain why our organizations ought need to innovate, being bold in taking on the innovation challenge build people's readiness and receptivity to change, assisting people to resolve their unconscious biases and resistance to it, developing both customer intimacy and customer empathy. However, although innovation can bring positive impact in a business, but it is so difficult to implement because new ideas and initiative depend on the people who work for the organizations. It is a lot harder to achieve desired results. Innovation is not about optimizing gross margins , but about attempt how finding new ways to create more value for yourselves profit image to attract more customers consideration.

Innovation is difficult to implement, because no system, process, or industry knows how to change, more innovations are worth exploring for many. Technology for example, can be re-purposed into new innovative solutions provide your customers with new value. The challenge is that when it comes to disruptive innovation, it almost always involves " higher risk" compared to incremental changes and thus can not be managed the same way as regular business projects are managed.

Hence, maintaining quality and product improvement and process development often involves standardization, whereas innovation can rarely be standardized . Also, new innovationds can not be measured using the same metrics and value drivers as the existing products and services . To overcome this major barrier to innovation, companies should approach disruptive innovation differently compared to how they are used to approaching regular projects. This, any organizations need to understand that they may fail to innovate. In the beginning, innovation and most specifically disruptive kind, is inferior to the existing products and services on the market. Because product improvement takes a lot of time and requires multiple iterations, the value for the customer at this point is minimal , when distuptive innovation initally caters only to a small and not so profitable customer base, established organizations are focused on serving more demanding, high and customers using their existing value channels. This is where it typically has higher profit margins, which is why established companies with rational decision-making processes usually choose not to invest in disruptive initiatives in the easrly stages. The problem ocurs when incumbents attempt to apply new technologies to trheir existing value networks or refuse moving into new markets because they are seen as too small to drive growth goals or are simply perceived to have too low margins. So, for organizations that prioritize reaching scale through operational efficiency, it makes more sense to focus on growing the business through incremental means, such as invest in risky and uncertain innovations.

On conclusion, in reality, however, organizations need to do both simultaneously improve the core business and exploit new business opportunities . Hence, when any organizations decide to innovate their product, or manufacturing processing or workplace . They need to find a balance between different types of innovations to choose which is the most effective innovation, which is a lot more sustainable may be stay in the business and to grow it is the long term to in order to implement innovation in success aim.

Chapter 4

Organizational technological innovaton

Which kinds of industries will be influenced by future (AI) technological development bring economy growth

What (AI) technological development will influence what kinds of UK and US industries development within ten years? Are environment and education and automatic manufacturing technologies will be UK and US future (AI) new technological development trends? What will be the difference between the (AI) developed countries and (non AI) developing countries future technologies development both in the future?

1 (AI) online teaching technology development

Future, (AI) online teaching method will be popular to be applied to teach to any university in possible, even secondary and primary schools. Because internet service is free charge to any students in any countries. Many different age students who can know how to apply internet as well as internet studying is very convenient to any students who can to internet to learn or study in home or public library or school library conveniently. Teachers do not need spend much time to teach students in classroom. They can use internet to teach teachers by face to face seeing and talking to their individual student from every student's computer. So, students do not also often spend much time to go to school to learn. So, developing any fast speed and time saving and talking and listening online teaching methods will be popular needs to any UK primary and secondary and university students in the future. It will be one new technological teaching method to change the traditional classroom educational method in UK and schools. For example, when one UK student who had left UK and is living in another country long time. If any UK school did not provide online teaching service to any UK students. It means that the UK citizen can not choose study himself/herself any UK school if who still hope to study any UK course when who is living in another country. Even one foreign student who does not go to UK to study, if he/she can find any UK primary or secondary or university to study from online. Then, the UK school won't lose one foreign student, due to it does not provide online teaching method to any foreign students. So, online Technology educational learning method will be one popular learning method which is enhanced, supported, mediated or assessed by the use of electronic media. Technology also enhanced learning may involve the use of new or established technology and/or the creation of new learning material. It may be deployed both locally and at a distance (i.e. a combination of traditional and e-learning approaches), to learning that is delivered entirely online. Online learning technology characteristics (features) include identification of a project lead for each area of any learning strategy, identification of two " quick win" for example lecture capture, electronic submission and feedback.

How can online technology enhance learning at UK any schools? It will include these several aspects to analyze. On identifying, prioritizing and innovation hand, online technology is a process for resourcing, prioritizing, acquiring and evaluating school software and hardware for UK any school needs. On staff development learning plan and a student skills development plan hand, UK schools need to establish a base-line policy on the standard (minimum) technology enhanced learning expectation for education each program and module and a mechanism for updating the schools' policies. On evaluation and research hand, a mechanism for engaging the owners of the technology enhanced learning strategy with best practice in the sector including contributing to and benefiting from pedagogical research and the evaluation of the student experience to UK any school.

Thus, UK schools can apply (AI) teachers to teach their students from online technological teaching channel to develop on educational aspect, such as (AI) teachers' digital literacies and appropriate technical skills that equip UK students for life-long learning, graduate level employment and professional practice, be empowered to learn how to learn with online teaching technology, using online technology to engage in interactive, creative and co-constructed learning with the potential for online learning in an interdisciplinary and international context, using online teaching technology to engage in learning with and from people from anywhere in the world, be supported on placement and in workplace learning through mobile applications and other supportive technologies that facilitate their online learning when away from the classroom, having access to innovative methods of online learning teaching and assessment that are the foundation of a research-lead academic environment, engaging with UK schools in developing , implementing and reviewing the technology enhanced learning strategy. Thus, in the future, it is important to build a capacity to apply (AI) teaching robots to teach their students from the online education technology to adopt future learning innovation and student individual online learning need (demand) to UK any school (AI) robotic online teaching trend.

There are many examples where UK academics working in isolation or in small UK teaching organizations or classroom learning groups have developed (AI) robotic teaching innovation that have a positive impact on UK students' academic experience , but these have remained isolated to particular modules or occasionally program. The aim of education researching online learning process is to identify the good (AI) robotic teachers' online teaching innovation that is being developed and to prioritize those that have the potential to make a significant contribution to improving the academic student experience at UK any schools. This online teaching process will need any UK schools which can plan how to apply limited resources necessary to achieve online teaching. In addition, the online teaching research process would evaluate and prioritize large scale educational software and hardware requests for primary, secondary and university students' requests. An important part to this process will be to ensure the integration of (AI) robotic teaching tools and their educational method to be applied to online educational products and packages that school staff and students regular use to make routine working and access as seamless as possible.

Decisions about school administrative online technologies should not be taken in isolation before assessing the impact on UK teaching staff. In addition, a range of techniques such as, (AI) robotic online expert facilitation, (AI) robotic coaching and peer support will be used to support individuals, groups or longer academic units, who are learning on major technology enhanced (AI) robotic teching online learning projects. Staff engagement may also facilitated through incorporating technology that is used in teaching staff research and/or professional activity that can be cooperated into their teaching.

Consequently, (AI) robotic online learning technology can develop UK students skills, UK schools need to understand how UK students understand technology and learn with it, therefore the digital literacy strategy needs to be considered as part of the overall strategy as well as the relevant skills development in UK employability strategy. So, in the future, (AI) teaching robotic online learning and teaching technology will make it clear that students will develop technical skills the appropriate level for graduate employability and professional practice. Also, in the future, the (AI) robotic teaching online technology can enhance learning working group to discuss external development, that are of educational strategic importance, understanding and evaluating current best practice and research and understanding and evaluating the online educational strategic contribution that pedagogical research and student feedback can have on online educational strategy, policy and practice. The (AI) robotic teaching e-learning unit is responsible for informing and educating. This could be done by, for example, providing a short digest of relevant information for each meeting and by setting aside a proportion of each school meeting to discuss a topic of particular (AI) robotic teachers to be applied to online educational strategic interest to every school. Academics that have not got a specialist interest in (AI) robotic teaching online educational technology enhanced learning will need relevant information at an appropriate time. This could be provided at a school department or faculty level and this will have clear links to the staff and (AI) robotic teaching online teaching development plan. Hence, future (AI) robotic teaching online educational development strategy will influence any UK or US educational school technological improvement in the future (AI) robotic online teaching method.

2 (AI) robotic environmental protection technology

Can future (AI) robotic environment technology be valid to human to develop? Nowadays, global air and water pollution is serious. For example, UK has many farming is polluted by the water and air pollution. It will influence UK farmers' income if whose farm land (natural resource) is polluted by water or air (natural resource). Even it will influence UK citizen will encounter food shortage if UK farmers can not grow any fresh and health food to provide the enough food numbers to eat every day. Moreover, air and water pollution will influence UK citizen drink the polluted water and breathe the dirty air to live every day. This natural resource (air and water challenge) will influence UK citizen health to cause illness , even death every easily. So, UK government can not neglect the natural environment pollution challenge. The environmental protection technology will help the UK and development countries to solve the challenge of climate change to avoid or reduce farming, foods, or vegetable or fruits or rice, pork, livestock numbers loss threats, i.e. the development and deployment of low carbon energy technology, including technology for the efficient use of energy. The commercialization of low carbon energy and energy efficiency technologies in the UK, with a specific focus on the demonstration and deployment phases of bringing low carbon technologies to UK market.

The UK Government needs to deliver a low carbon economy and to meet UK ambitions emission reduction target. So, low carbon and environmental protection technology researching and development will reduce the carbon intensity of energy production as well as reduce energy demand, towards meeting the contributing UK's ambitions production as well as reduce energy demand, and renewable energy goals. The use of energy (including transportation fuel) and the UK's targets on climate change, for example, by helping the UK make a step change in increasing deployment of renewable energy, improving UK energy efficiency and helping low carbon technologies reach the market. The development of low carbon technologies, and to realize the benefits of doing so in terms ensuring security of energy supply for the UK future economy development.

In UK, private sector investment in technology innovation in the low carbon energy sector will other sectors of the economy. So, in UK energy technologies are likely needed to be developed to avoid dangerous climate change, or an acceptable cost. So, in the future, UK government will need to consider to research environment protection and low carbon energy technology. The activities will reduce carbon emissions, or have the potential to reduce carbon emissions on the longer term, through the use of energy technology will accelerate development and deployment of low-carbon energy and energy efficiency technologies will capacity in the demonstration and deployment of low carbon technologies. Innovation in the energy sector is the only way to identify, develop and reduce the costs of new and improved technologies for the extractions, generation, distribution and use of energy. It has long been an important means of achieving the UK's energy policy aims of a secure and affordable energy supply, as well as to develop the environmentally friendly technologies that are required in UK response to climate change, i.e. nuclear, wind or water, sun energy technology, which is future new energy technology is suitable to research to create to apply instead of current electricity energy.

How global warming influences UK agriculture growth. Scientists have also been fighting the use of chlorine in municipal water systems to kill various strands of bacteria. Chlorine reduces by about 80% the number of alimentary tract diseases relative to polluted, unchlorinated water. A relatively new genetically modified agricultural products. They were partly successful in Europe, such as UK (some countries banned genetically modified products) in spite of the fact that neither history nor research supports their case. People began to modify plants as early as the beginning of the agricultural revolution (8000 to 10,000 years ago), when they started seed selection and who have continued ever since. The green revolution of the 1960 year brought about strains of grans and rice more resistant to a variety of local conditions. The effects have been that countries like India, which had suffered from recurrent famines over the millennia, became self-sufficient in food due to the resultant sharp increase in agricultural productivity. It was a real science and technology over the poverty dominating most of human history. But it is precisely the products of science and technology that ecologists are so deathly afraid of. In an interesting study in a quarter (28%) of clinically analyzed cases of obsessive compulsive disorder were cases resulting from the fear of global warming.

To destroy the modern, whether industrial or postindustrial, civilization, human have to destroy an important engine of economic growth, that is its energy sources. And this is what eco-warriors try to achieve under the banner of against global warming. Thus, UK government will have responsibility to attempt to research new technology to fight global warming challenge for itself farmer benefits and even global benefits both on the future.

Hence, future (AI) robotic development can be applied to environment protection aspect. Future (AI) robotic tools can help human to predict when and how any why environment pollution will occur in which countries and (AI) robotic tools can be one environment protection machine to gather environment pollution information to give opinions to human how we ought need to do in anywhere in order to avoid the places' environment pollution will become serious in influence our health. So, future (AI) robotic machince will be one predictive environmental pollution and bad climate change machine and it can give opinions to avoid serious environment pollution and give solutions to solve environment pollution any country.

(AI) will give global warming technological protection economic influence opinion to human

Some future economists indicated reasons to explain why UK government and businessmen needed to consider how to develop natural environment protection technology to avoid global warming challenge to influence UK economy development. They indicated the anthropogenic (human-made) global warming resulting from the increase in "greenhouse gas". They offered their perspectives on the scientific valid of anthropogenic global warming phenomenon, its probability of occur and expected consequences and is dominated by technologists, economists and political scientists, who considered the need to make the horribly costly adjustments in energy generation and usage suggested by climate alarmists.

Many stress that global warming is primarily caused by other phenomena than human use of fossil fuels or human activities in general. They are looking at the activities of the sun and impact of the larger universe as the main source of global warming and stress that global warmings (plural) happen intermittently with global cooling. I shall explain why global climate warming will influence to the political and economics of the issue to UK country. For it is the latter, rather than the global warming itself, that will pose a challenge to the Western world, such as UK and the world at large in the future. Scientists concerned who should move forward with policy measures to avert the alleged disaster. They also apply manufacturing theories to support enough to frighten politicians into action and scare societies into acceptance of measures that would sharply reduce UK citizen their living standards. Otherwise, UK politicians had support that bureaucracies were established, money allocated and lobbies created dependent on the new kind of subsidies. In consequences, climate alarmism and resultant interventions in national economies and human activities have become the increasingly wide spread and increasingly cost reality. With the growing availability of money distributed, and even more promised, a range of benefit of the global warming machinery has been on the increase. So, if UK government did not concern how to innovate new weather protection technology to avoid climate change adverse (poor) influence. It is possible that billions of dollars of UK public money are needed to spend on research global warming challenge because global warming will influence UK agricultural industry. UK agricultural industry is one important export income source to raise UK GDP income every year. If global warming become very serious to influence UK weather to be bad to cause UK farmers who can not grow good taste food and vegetable to supply to domestic and overseas food consumers to eat. Then, UK will loss much GDP income from local agricultural export sale. It seems global warming and agricultural production which has direct relationship to influence UK economy development in the future.

The main problem with climatology is that it must be based as already stressed on very many variables affecting climate and too few hard data necessity. Differences apply not only with respect to the scale of changes obtained, but even to their direction (rising or declining temperature). Some weather scientists indicated to concern global warming challenge. In consequence, it would be impossible to discover if and where errors were made not only in estimating relationships between variables but also in the quality of data used. (Hauser, J. Tellis, G. J; Griffin, A. 2006) They were comparing average temperatures measured some 30, 40 or 50 years ago by, say, 90 % weather stations in the countryside and 10 % stations in the cities with contemporary average temperatures measured by weather stations located today on 50:50 basis in the countryside and cities. Then, one could obtain the increasing temperatures without any real world climate or even weather changes. Comparability would be ensured if the same number of countryside-located and city-located weather stations had been compared for different periods. The alarmists intentionally mix up " temperature growth" with the trend of temperature growth. To give an example, if in the first decade the temperature grew by 0.5 % degree, in second decade it grew by 0.3 % and in third decade it grew by 0.1%, what was registered was a growth in the temperature, but certainly not a trend of growing temperature. A fourth decade should, on the basis of the trend, bring about no change in the temperature.

To conclude, scientists believed that global warming was caused by human's bad behavior more than natural environment influence. So, it is human's responsibility needs to solve this challenge, due to who feel earning profit aim is more important to protect natural environment, e.g. air and water pollution , due to manufacturing process is the main factor. So, UK has responsibility to attempt to research how to solve global warming challenge , such as it has many famous scientists who can devote their scientific skills to cooperate to solve global warming challenge with other countries' scientists. Some weather scientists also hypothesized that human may be at the end of the present warming period. If they are right, it would be bad for humanity, as warmer periods have always been associated with better conditions for economic activity. To sum up, scientists believed that global warming will influence human economic activity to be bad.

Future (AI) robotic environmental protection machine can give opinions to UK farmers:

Climate alarmists were able to convince a large part of the Western public and a majority of Western politicians of the cause of fighting against the global warming. It supposes itself in an instinctive preference for collectivist solutions in economic and social spheres, with negative to disastrous consequences when scientists are applied in practice, so UK government needs to concern global warming challenge, due to it is possible that it will influence UK natural environment weather to be poor to influence many UK farmers' agricultural and vegetable and fruit and rice wheat etc. food growth successfully. What is the global warming influence to cause disease? For example, ecological alarmists and activists (eco-warriors) never admit they are wrong, they long pursued their fear mongering campaign against chlorine. Their success in branding DDT a dangerous substance had a negative impact on the malaria eradication campaign in poorer parts of the world. Alternatives to be have been far less effective and the result has been the resurgence of malaria cases and the manifold increase in malaria -caused deaths to the largest extent in Africa.

3 (AI) robotic automation technology in manufacturing industry

Future, (AI) robotic automation technology can be applied to manufacturing industry. For example, nowadays, UK computer and space explore technology had reached the mature stage. It means that UK government ought not need to continue spend much resource to research these two kind technologies. Otherwise, the (AI)robotic automatic manufacturing technology, e.g. human intelligence new product. It has need to develop because human intelligence machines will bring beneficial to satisfy human everyday life need, e.g. hospital patients' activities need, if the patent who can not walk easily, but the human intelligence machine can assist the patient walk to anywhere conveniently. So, he/she does not need to sit on wheel chair and apply the human intelligence machine man to help him/her to drive on the intelligence automatic driving vehicle to go to anywhere conveniently.

Otherwise, increased automation in low wage countries, e.g. China, Korea, Africa, Hong Kong etc. which have traditionally manufacturing firms, could use automatic technological manufacturing to bring lose cost advantage and potentially lose their ability of achieving rapid economy growth by shifting workers to factory jobs. So, UK government and businessmen needs to consider automation technology development, i.e. 3D printing manufacturing industry will encourage UK companies to move manufacturing process, closer to gain the biggest advantage from this 3D automation technology development.

A growing concern of premature de-industrialization in energy and developing countries could require new models and a need un-skillful the UK workforce. In the future, the best way toward for UK cities will reduce their exposure to automation is to boost their technological dynamic and attract more UK skilled workers. Automation technology progress can give UK manufacturers' employee benefits, such as long term healthy productivity improvement, raising productivity efficiency and product quality, macroeconomic and microeconomic effects of automation technological change, it's change will be beneficial to UK society, i.e. automation active labor market policies, which could help UK job seekers find jobs from training to incentive to support self-employment to create high technological job employment chance in UK society. So, raising science, technology, engineering and math subjects update skills level are needed to UK any universities, which can be increasingly important in UK society, these factors could complicate the ability of UK high automation technology education to adopt to the UK automation manufacturing technological change. A talent mismatch already exists in UK, with many well UK educated workers can find employment in lower-skilled jobs. To combat this, greater coordination will be needed between the education, training and employment sectors in UK society.

Why are high automatic technology product development models needed to research to UK any manufacturers? UK government and manufacturers need to consider how to achieve high technology product development models. According to Hauser et al. (2006) indicated the high technology (high tech.) development process, is influenced by the innovative process, bringing products on exception value which stimulate product market demand. Innovation provides products the specific basis for which world economies compete with each other on the global market. Able to find new solutions, innovations generate significant changes in existing markets, destroy them, or create new marketing (Hauser et al. 2006). So, UK manufacturers need to concern on any manufacturing high technology product development process because which can influence any new products development to manufacture to sell to any overseas or domestic both markets successfully.

What is high tech. product meaning? Mohr et al. (2010) argues that there are two reasons why it is important to clarify and specific high technology : (1) due to the impact of technologies on the economy, attempts are made to classify economic production and incomes ; (2) due to the impact of high tech. on the environment. Standard marketing strategies are being modified and adopted , therefore, it is necessary to know the products to focus on. Why UK manufacturers need to consider high technological product process. Nowadays, high tech. products are complex, advanced, requiring specific technical knowledge, which is technologically not discontinued and being produced at the companies which have twice as many technical personnel and invest twice as many in scientific research and development than other companies. Moreover, these products are time-sensitive as scientists are continuously searching for new approaches for invention of more advanced technologies which make all preceding ones lower-ranking. The most important, nowadays global consumers will adopt the particular technology. It means that global customers may delay adopting new high-tech. products and in order to mitigate the prolonged uncertainty require a high degree of education and information about the product and need post-purchase reassurance.

Anyway, nowadays customer individual needs in high tech. environments are characterized by sudden changes related to unpredictable fashion. Even, consumers concern about how to preserve new product‘ competitive technological standard is completely incompatible with technological uncertainty. The most important factor is the prevalence rate of any new products development process, which is influenced by slower than of traditional products. In many cases high-tech. automatic product market are being materialized slower than which are expected. The technological uncertainty challenges will exist in development process, such as uncertainty related to the timetable for development of the question whether the new product will be function as promised. In automatic high-tech. industries, the time requires for product development is difficult to predict as , commonly, it takes longer than expected , uncertainty related to unanticipated consequences and uncertainty about the product life cycle related to competition products. In conclusion, these factors will influence new automatic technology product development process unsuccessful, so UK manufacturers will need to concern on any high technological automatic product's manufacturing process.

Future economists predict automatic technology how to influence future UK economy

Before, all over the world presented picture of demonstrate in London on the occasion of the meeting of the G20. Some economists indicated disastrous economy consequences will occur to any one of Western country , such as UK, so if any one of Western country did not consider automatic technology development to itself country. They indicated one example, such as material incentives to produce disappeared throughout Russia and, when Society leadership called off the experiment, the country faced industrial output reduced to 10% of what had been registered in 1914 and agricultural output reduced to such low levels as to cause widespread famine.

Why would UK encounter disastrous economy consequences if UK government did not encourage manufacturers spend money to invest to innovate automatic technology industry? According to a variety of anthropological studies, a collectivity is unable to operate efficiently with everybody giving talent workers have chance to devote whose best effort to manufacture any high technological products, e.g. human intelligence vehicle or airplane. Hence, economic incentives are needed to UK manufacturers to invest high technological automatic industry development. Because the economists predict UK will have many talent worker numbers, their number will be more than a certain number of normal effort workers, due to UK technological education level is very excellent to provide to train many young technological manufacturing students to find this kind of high technological manufacturing job. So, the high technological manufacturing job seekers will increase and it won't decrease to UK job market in the future.

Assuming that UK high technological automatic manufacturing workers who would desire only to introduce changes in the workings of the international economic order and policies of countries participating in the present economic order rather than change the order itself, what will be UK manufacturers their specific economic preferences in the future? It implies tnat either concentrate on spending more investment to automatic high technological development, e.g. human intelligence automatic high technological products or still concentrate on spending more investment to common traditional technological products.

However, UK was a developed Western country which had had strong automatic high technological development effort very long time. Otherwise, it compared to some developing countries, such as Asian China, Hong Kong, Korea etc. Asian countries their future economic growth rate will show un- surprising , different patterns, so the Asian countries has weak effort to invest high automatic technological product development, such as human intelligence technological development. The catching-up process suggests low economic growth rate in the high automatic technological product development to the Asian developing countries in the future.

Hence, the future economists predict that it views as probable successors of the Western world economic leadership if any Western country , such as UK manufacturers who prefer to invest to any high automatic technological products development , e.g. developing on human intelligence automatic technological products more than traditional common technological products development. On the one side, but it seems important to stress that two very poor countries among the challengers-China and India-are examples of countries that changed their institutions and economic policies from no or little economic freedom to more economic freedom. Because there two countries whose governments prefer to lend loans to encourage their country manufacturers prefer to invest high automatic technological products manufacturing. On the other side, attitudes toward foreign direct investment (FDI) have undergone change since the 1960 s and a large majority of less developed countries, e.g. China and India are now competing strongly among themselves and with developed market economies for direct investment from multinational companies. So, UK will face China and India high automatic technological product competitors in the future. And in fact, all countries that joined Western developed economies did that without much (if any) external inflow of public resources. It is right time that UK government needs to lend loans to encourage domestic manufacturers to invest high automatic technological products to raise whose international high technological products sale effort to win its future competitors. So, machine resources will be increased demand to o UK manufacturers if who chose to spend machine resources to innovate to manufacture any new and high technological automatic products to raise human daily life needs in the future. It means that it is right time UK manufacturers need buy much machines to prepare to manufacture many future high technological automatic products when these machine prices are low. Because the future global machine prices will possible be raised if many China and India manufacturers will also buy many machines in the future. For example, USA government had provided much financial support to assist sugar cane producers to develop their businesses. And they are dependent to a much larger extent than sugar cane producers and sugar processors in the USA on government. Without very high subsidies to renewable energy generation, they would not have survived at all. So, USA government had been the first country which could lent much financial assistance to encourage domestic renewable energy generation manufacturers to develop high technological energy manufacturing business. So, UK government needs follow USA to lend financial assistance to encourage domestic high technological automatic industry development. Future economists also predict China and India will be competitors for future leadership in the global economy, special high technological products. China has been the media and analyst's favorite for quite some time. Quantitative projections have seemingly supported such expectation. Such as China and India had manufactured many high technological new space rockets products, ocean war large ships etc. Moreover, China has become one of the major world trade players in the early twenty-first century.

Many long-term forecasts, assuming similarly high economic growth rates in the decades ahead, predict that China will surpass the USA in terms of aggregate GDP somewhere between 2020 and 2030 or later, say between 2030 and 2050 year. The future economists conclude on the basis of these predictions that China will not only pass the USA in aggregate product (GDP), but its economy and economic policies will influence the rest of the world to a similar extent that the USA does at present.

I stressed a very important point, namely that the UK future high technological automatic product competitor China and India, namely that economies not only grow, but in the process change their structure. China and India have been industry very rapidly (the first transition) and building the physical infrastructure that accompanies industrialization changes to technology in the future. However, at a certain per capita GNP level the two countries, such as China and India will face another structural shift when which technological development will reach the mature stage in the future. China and India had been primarily historical pattern of economic development because the shift in the role of engine of growth from industry to services is to a much greater extent a qualitative shift. Both higher and different skills are required. And, even more importantly, interactions generating ideas driving the highly human-capital-intensive service economy require a much freer environment, not only in the economic area. Chinese exports have been heavily labor-intensive. This being the case, they contributed to the expansion of industrial employment, offering for the first time in the history of China a taste of (very modest) prosperity to more than 100 million new industrial workers and their families. This is the major component of the success accomplished by Chinese economic growth. Richer trade partners create room for more trade, so the Chinese should hope that intra-South trade, that is, trade between the emerging economies of Asia, the Middle East, Africa and Latin America, will open up new and growing opportunities. I presume that if Western economy , such as UK did not developed high technological automatic industry to stable their social welfare, so thoroughly slowed down their economic growth.

Will it allow China to accomplish the transition to a mature, innovation, service-sector-based market economy? It has allowed the economy to industrialize much more successfully, even if the labor shift from agriculture to industry has not yet been completed. But it is a long way off the next major test: the second high technological industry transition of the economic structure to China. Bear in mind that Russia attempted it twice and failed at both attempts.

But even, assuming that China at some point in the future does succeed in accomplishing the second transition, will it be able to supersede the USA, for example, as the main global high automatic technological innovation center if it wants to become the No.1 global high technological industry economy? Given the nature of the centralized state and its stability to collect financial resources , China's ability to increase research and development expenditure to high automatic technological products and to hire a mass of researchers, engineers, technicians and other specialists should not be doubted. This process in already taking place.

But , again, Soviet Russia already exceed the USA in the R&D/GDP ratio in the 1970s, long before the communist collapse, with no effects on its innovativeness. Inputs matter less than outputs, quantity in the innovation process mean much less than quality. The latter characteristics depends importantly on economic, civic and even political institutions. Otherwise, independent India had three options open to it in 1946s. It could pursue spontaneous economic development, with some state intervention to be sure, along the lines of basically free market capitalism; it could turn the clock back and try to recreate the rural-agricultural and handicraft based. The dominant way of thinking was Society -style priority to industrialization and , within industralization , priority to heavy industry. In other words, not textiles and clothing, which has been developing well in India since the mid- nine teen century, but production of sewing machines and , even better, production of machines the produce sewing machines.

The results were only to be expected. The heavy stress on the expansion of capital-intensive heavy industries in a very poor country quickly strained the ability of the Indian economy to generate adequate savings. Moreover, some of these industries were above the level of industrial competence of an underdeveloped economy. Thus, the amount of required resources (capital, skilled labor) was usually larger per unit of output than in the same industries in more mature, richer industries economies. In another view point, India will develop light industries, just as any other poor country with a great deal of unskilled labor, had a comparative advantage and no less importantly, an economy in which, due to their low capital/labor ratio, light industries could employ many more people, spreading prosperity more widely in a poor country. So, it explain that why China will have more effort to develop heavy high technological industry in the future. Thus, India got less economic efficiency, less employment than in a spontaneously developing economy, less ability to compete internationally in light industries suitable for an underdeveloped economy and finally got heavy industry unable to compete even on the domestic market and, therefore requiring no less heavy a dose of protection. Overall India got an underperforming economy, in particular in its relations with the rest of the world.

To conclude by comparing the performance of the traditional sectors of the Indian economy and the performance of its modern, human -capital-intensive subsector of manufacturing and skill intensive service sector. The latter both employ workers with high-and medium -high skillful level (in branches ranging from computer software and biotechnology and pharmaceutical high technological light industry). India is ahead of China in terms of the output and export of such products and services. Thus, it implies that UK ought concentrate on developing high automatic heavy high technological industry, e.g. human intelligence technological products because these industry is not better development to other many countries' strong effort , such China and India large population countries.

Consequently, future (AI) robotic technology can be applied to medical service industry, e.g. in hospital and clinic environment to let patients to live in these places to feel more comfortable. It can also be applied to manufacturing industry to assist productivity performance rasing and computer software and biotechnology and pharmaceutical high technological light industry to improve computer technological software development and invention of much new biotechnology and pharmaceutical medicines for human health.

4 Increase development in genetics, human intelligence, robotics, nanotechnology, 3D printing and biotechnology technological industry

In US future, (AI) robotic tools will assist nanotechnology, 3D printing and biotechnology technological industry development, these kinds of jobs will be needed to increase development in genetics, human intelligence, robotics, nanotechnology, 3D printing and biotechnology. For example, smart systems homes, factories, farms grids or cities will help tackle problems ranging from supply chain management to climate change. The rise of US economy growth will allow US people to monetize everything from their empty house to their car in US. These new technological products development will change US patterns of consumption, production and employment adaption are also be changed by US corporations, US government and individuals.

Why will the technological revolution be broader socio-economic, geopolitical and demographic drivers of change to influence future US social economic and consumption pattern change? Future US most occupations will also be changed. When some traditional old jobs are threatened by redundancy and other new technological jobs will grow rapidly, existing jobs are also changed in the skill sets required to do them. The debate is between some economists foresee limitless new job opportunities and foresee massive dislocation of US jobs. In fact, the reality is highly specific to future US high technological production industry, region and high technological occupation in question as well as how US production workers can be raised themselves ability to actions the upgrade level of high technological production ability from various stakeholders to manage high technological production method change.

Overall, this is a modestly positive outlook of US high technological production employment across future most high technological production industries with jobs growth expected in several sectors. However, it is also clear that this need for more talent in certain job categories is accompanied by high skills instability across all job categories. Combined together, future US net job growth and skills instability result in most US businesses with face major recruitment challenges and talent shortages, a pattern already evident in the result and set to get worse over next five years in possible.

The question is how US businesses, government and individuals will react to these new technological job changes, due to talent shortage, mass unemployment and growing inequality challenges will encounter in future US society.

The current technological revolution does not need become a race between humans and machines , but rather an opportunity for work to truly become a channel through which US people recognize their potential. So, if US traditional low manufacturing skillful workers lack talent to learn new skills to prepare to do future new technological manufacturing jobs, such as 3 D printing, robotics, nanotechnology, biotechnological high technological products manufacturing jobs. Then, it will cause increasing of unemployment rate to some not talent US low manufacturing skillful workers. So, US government or high technological product industry employers need to consider this future unemployment challenge will be caused by high technological products manufacturing changing influences. It seems high technological development will cause these low manufacturing skillful workers unemployed rising numbers as well as high manufacturing skillful workers human capital shortage global challenges will exist.

In the future, the driver of changes to influence US demographic and socio-economic growth. They may include: changing work environments and flexible working arrangements. It means new technologies are enabling workplace innovations , such as remote working, co-working spaces and teleconferencing. Rising of the middle class in Asia markets. It means the world's economic center is shifting towards the Asia developing countries.

Some economists predict that Asia will be projected to account for 66% of the global middle class and for 59% of middle class consumption by 2030 year. In addition, climate change, natural resource will be constraints to a greener economy. It means that climate change is a major driver of innovation as organizations search for measures to help adjust to its effects. As global economic growth consumers are needed to lead to demand for natural resources and raw materials, over explanation implies higher extraction most and degradation ecosystem and these challenges will also impact US employment changes needs. All US government also needs to concern future global economic change influence. Hence , future (AI) robotic tools will assist these industries' technological development and creates more new jobs.

CHAPTER IV

Organizational technological innovaton

(AI) assist future computer
industry new gender innovation development

Why China's computer manufacturing and product development industry will be global leader to compete US computer dominant market. The reason is because that China will have possible to dominate global computer industry development if it can invent new (AI) learning tool to assist global computer systems to raise more efficient performance effort.
Nowadays, China's computer industry is the largetest hardware producer production and experts is dominated by Taiwanese firms. It is also the second largest personal computer (pc) market and domestic pc companies are top three sellers in global computer manufacturing and product development market. Forx example, Lenovo buys BM pc business in 2004 year. It implies US, IBM pc manufacturing leader can not dominate global computer market in possible in the future.
Reed Electronic Research, Yearbook Of World Electronic Data (2003) indicated that the leading computer producing countries of hardware production in US $millions and share share of total gogal production: The world region US was the global rank number one. In 1995 year, US had US $76,284 value, market value 26.5%. Then in 2000 year, US had increased up to US $ 90, 430 value, market share 24%. Till to 2003 year, US had fallen down to US $ 69,102 value, market share 21.7%. However, US hardware production was still the global rank number one , although its hardware production value had been falling down. But, the following second rank country, Japan and the third rank country, Singapore and the fourth rank country, Taiwan and the fifth rank county China which hardware production value could not exceed US till to 2003 year. However, although China had the lowest hardware production value US $5,600 to compare to among of these countries in 1995 year, but China had increased the value to US $65,000 and market share to 20.5%. Otherwise, Japan, Singapore and Taiwan value and market share had surprisingly fallen down below than China value in 2003 year. Thus, it seemed that China will be a potential country to compete US hardware production industry after 2003 year.

Reed Electronic Research, Year book Of World Electronic Data (2003) also showed that these computer companies of China had these % of market share : Beijing Founder had 9.9%, Tsinghua Tongtang had 7.8%, dell had 7.2 % , IBM had 5.1% , HP had 4.8% of market share. Thus, it also seemed that China some computer companies will have impotant large market share percentage in global pc sale market. In the future, global hardware production and pc sale industry. China and Taiwan both countries will be one pc manufacturing and design and sale partner. The reason is that China and Taiwan had been the number one rank of markers of notebook pcs, motherboards, scanners, keyboards, add-on card optical drives, monitors and some network equipment etc. pc (personal computer) relative computer function products. It seems that these both countries had co-operated to research any computer relative products to sell to global computer market. They are also the original design manufacturers (DDMS) develop and manufacture over half the world's notebook pcs as well as their customers include all major branded pc vendors (OEMS).

Taiwan Minstry Of Economic Affairs (2003) indicated Taiwan's top notebook ODMS include: In 2003 year volume (thousands) Quanta had $8,500 sale volume thousands , for example, Quanta major OEM partners include Gateway, Dell, HP, IBM, Apple , Sharp, Sony, Fujitsu-Siemens (F/S). Compal had $6,000 sale volume (thousands) , Compal major OEM partners include Dell, HP, F/S, Toshiba, Acer. Thus, it also implied Taiwan had many small size and non famous brand of computer companies which choose to co-operate to be partners with some global large size and famous brand of computer companies to raise competitive effort in global computer market, such as Dell, IBM, HP, Gatway, Apple etc.

Thus, the future trend of computer new product manufacturing development will shift from US to Taiwan and SE Asia, then to China. However, what kind of knowledge work factors will be needed to China and Taiwan . In general, notebook manufacturing stages will include: The first process is design stage, it includes concept design, such as analyze need, create concept and set brand image as well as product planning, such as business case, specifications, industrial design and sourcing strategy. The second process is development stage, it includes design review steps, such as design review, such as mock-ups, electrical test as well as prototype build, such as commercial samples, integrated system test as well as pilot production, such as production process design, pilot. Final process is production stage, it includes mass production, such as ramp-up, volume production, production testing and global distribution as well as sustaining support, such as speed bump, component replacement, technical support and warranty support. Thus, I believe that China and Taiwan must own thee knowledge work skillful of computer design and development professionals who can assist these two countries how to innovate their future computer development to change global traditional computer model to be renew and innovate computer model in the future.

Due to computer industry's stages of development and manufacturing are closely linked , need manufacturability , testing of sample products, concept design and product planning stay together in lead markets and branded vendors, design and development can be separated organizationally and geographically. Thus, China and Taiwan choose to co-operate to exchange their different skill, such as either China has own more concept design and product planning skill or more development skill or more production skill. Then, China will choose either one of the most beneficial comparative advantage among of them. To bring this one of the most beneficial co-operative advantage to attract Taiwan to choose either one of the beneficial comparative advantage of skill, such as either design or development or producton to already co-operate to compete the Western developed country US together.

Thus, US won't be the global computer industry development leader if both US country famous and large employee number computer companies, such as IBM and Apple which choose to outsource their pc design and development and production skill to China and Taiwan both countries to help them to develop global computer design and development and production skill to be upgraded. Thus, I feel these both countries will plan how to co-operate to compete US to win the global computer industry leader position in the future.

When China invented its (AI) learning system success. Why does it influence global computer industry market change? For example, in the future, instead of global computer manufacters need to consider the design, development and production processes, who also need to consider what factors can influence consumers' laptop purchases. Because any consumers have much different computer model and brand to choose to make final decision to buy any computers. If the computer manufacturer can predict what factors will be whose weakness(es) to influence global computer consumers to change whose mind or attitude to choose to buy other brands of computers, then it won't lose its many old computer customer numbers

and reduces it market share in global computer market share.
Nowadays, in general computer has three kinds to provide to global consumers to choose to buy , such as laptop, notebook computers, desktops. it seems that laptop and notebook computers and desktops will have different factors to influence any consumers to choose to buy any brand of computer products. Thus, computer indsutry can divide three consumer groups, such as (stayers, satisfied switchers and dissatisfied switchers) of a computer company with respect to the factors influencing consumers' laptops or notebook computers or desktops purchases. However, I feel the factors can include such as core technicl features, post purchase services, prices and payment conditions, peripheral specification, physical appearance, value added features and connectivity and mobility seven main factors that are influencing consumers' laptop or notebook computer or desktop purchases in global computer industry market.
Ganesh et al., (2000) indicates the customer base of a company consists of three groups of consumers: stayers, satisfied switchers and dissatisfied switchers. Therefore, the consumers in this study replied to the question about whether the current brand that who were using was their first laptop brand or whether who had switched from a previous laptop brand. As a following question, consumers who had switched were asked to state the reason of why who switched from a previous laptop brand brand to their current brand. The options include overall dissatisfaction from the previous laptop brand and reasons other than dissatisfaction. Thus, computer companies need to know what factors influence either whose prior computer customers why who don't choose repeat to buy its any computer products or whose new potential computer customers why who don't choose to buy its any computer products in the first time choice. Thus, future computer manufacturers need to consider intangible salespeople service attitude or performance, such as salespeople current purchase and post purchase service, e.g. technical repair, model function explanation how to use the computer, instead of tangible product performance, e.g. computer appearance design , function , mobility and internet and document download speed connectivity function. Because salespeople and technicians' service performance can be represented to the computer image. If they can provide excellent service to let computer buyers to feel satisfactory, then they can help their computer company employer to build good image. So, staff service performance will be one important factor to influence computer consumers to make the final decision to choose

to buy the brand of computer products more easily. Even, one famous brand computer company, such as IBM, Apple, Gateway, these any one of famous brand computer company must not attract any new (the first time) or repeat computer buyers to choose to buy their any kind of computer products , such as laptop, desktop or notebook more easily due to their famous brand. Althoug, these famous computer companies had built good image to let consumers have more confidence to buy any kind of their computer products. But, if these famous computer companies‘ salepeople or repair technicians can not provide excellent customer service or performance to satisfy their computer buyers' service need, e.g. explaining how to use the new computer, repair post purchase service etc. I believe these famous brands of computer consumers will not have more desire to prefer to chose to buy any one of these famous computer brand's products. Otherwise, if the other less famous computer companies‘ any kind of laptop, desktop or notebook sale price is higher than the famous brand of computer companies' products sale price, but their salepeople or technicians can provide more excellent service attitude or performance to satisfy their consumers‘ needs. It is possible that the new or first time computer buyers or repeat computer buyers will still choose to buy their computers. So, the famous or less famous computer brand is not one important factor to influence the computer buyer to decide either to buy the computer or not buy the computer. Otherwise, computer company's salepeople and repair technician whose service performance or attitude will be one important intangible factors to influence any first time (new) or repeat computer consumers to choose to buy any famous or less famous brand of computer company's product, instead of the tangible computer design appearance and reliable function and convenient mobility and long term durability etc. factors influences.

Thus, China has possible to influence global office and home computer comsumers to choose to buy its any brands of computers to use if it can invent (AI) learning systems to assist global computers to raise their performance efficiency. So, it will influence global computer consumers to choose its country's any brands of computers to buy to use, due to themselves new (AI) learning computers can help office and home computer users to raise efficiency and provide the excellent productive performance to them more than the traditional computers.

1 Can culture factor influence the (AI) computer consumer choice?

When China's (AI) computer learning system has developed in success. Then, it will possible to influence global consumers' traditional computer applying culture to change to new innovation (AI) learning computer applying culture. It means that China will dominate global computer consumer choice to be trended to choose to buy China's any computer brands' produducts , due to it 's (AI) technology can be invented to apply to traditional computers in order to raise their efficiency and reduce office staffs' workload and provide excellent performance to serve office or home (AI) learning computer users.

Durmza and Zengin, (2011:53) indicted marketers closely interested in this issue to know the family which changed and renewed in course in time. It provides an advantage for a marketer to know the family structure and its consumption characteristics. Nowadays, consumer behavior is influenced not only by consumer personalities and motivation, but also by the relationships within families. Family is a social group and it can be considered a crucial place in th perception of marketing (Durmaz, Yakup, CELLK, Mucahit and ORUC, Reyhan, (2011).

The consumer buying behaviors examined through an empirical study. Then, it brings this question: Whether cultural factors will influnece the computer consumer choice. Choice and include computer brand choice, computer price choice, computer model choice, computer design choice, laptop or desktop or notebook product choice, new or second-hand old computer choice, the computer of manufacturing country choice, computer package choice etc. So, any consumer will consider to choose any one of these to decide to buy which kind of computer.

Every country computer consumers had different culture to influence their computer shopping choice. I feel culture can be explained how to influence to computer shopping such as: How do the country computer consumers buy and use their computer products habitually ? How do the country computer consumers react to th computer price changes, attractive advertising methods to satisfy whose needs and computer company store interiors? What underlying mechanisms operate to produce any one of the country computer consumers' responses? If computer marketers have answers to such these questions, who can make better managerial decisions how to adopt which computer target country (countries) consumers' culture.

Consumer behavior deals with many other issues, for instance (Priest, Carter and Statt, 2013: 19). How do we get information about products?

How do we assess alternative products? How do different people choose or use different products? How do we decide on value for money ? How much risk do we take with what products? Who influences our buying decisions and our use of the product? How are brand loyalties formed and changed? For computer industry, it means that how computer consumers get information about computer products, how computer consumers assess alternative notebook, desktop, laptop computer products, how different age, country, culture, sex, student or working people or retired people computer consumers choose or use different kind of computer products, such as notebook, desktop, laptop computer products, how much risk computer consumers take with notebook, desktop, laptop computer products, the computer consumers‘ buying decisons and their use of the desktop or notebook or laptop computer products will be influenced by whom, e.g. family, friends, teacher, employer, computer salepeople, advertisement marketer etc. , computer company brands how are formed and changed by whom, e.g. computer consumers, computer company competitors, marketers, different countries' culture etc.

Durmaz and Jablonski, (2012:56) also explained culture is the essential character of a society that distinguishes it from other cultural groups. The underlying elements of every culture are the values, language, myths, customs, laws and the artifacts or products that are transmitted from one generation to the next (Lamb, Hair and Deniel, 2011: 371). Culture is the most fundamental determinant of a person's wants and behavior. Whereas, lower creatives are governed by instinct, human behavior is largely learned. The child growing up in a society leans a basic set of values, perceptions, preferences and behaviors through a process of socialization involving the family and other social roles. So, I feel different country have different culture to influence as well as different country computer consumers who have different computer purchase and consume habitually. So, computer manufacturers ought focus on manufacturing the unique need and characteristics to satisfy any country's consumers‘ needs.

What is my idea about future global computer competition and factors influence computer consumer behavior ?

In conclusion, future computer industry development will trend that computer manufacturers need to consider every country's computer comsumer culture. Because every country computer consumers who will have different computer consumption habitually if who can predict what the country most computer consumers culture, then they can have more confidence to sell their computers to different country markets. Moreover, US computer manufacturers need to consider China and Taiwan computer manufacturing technology because it is possible that these both countries will be its main competitor among different computer manufacuring countries. Because thess both countries will cooperate to research new model of different computers to attract global computer consumers to choose to buy their new model of computer products in the future. Finally, computer manufacturers need to consider salepspeople and repair technicians service performance because computer consumers will consider intangible service performance , instead of tangible computer quality and price and style etc. factors . The main reason is that any computer have chance to be needed to repair and salespeople' skill will influence the computer consumer to make final decision to choose to buy the brand of computer. Thus, these factors will influence global computer development and trend in the future.

Artificial Intelligent Robot: Technology change traditional production of factor model

1 What is mean of (AI) Technological innovation production of factor ?

Can (AI) robot technological learning system change future traditional production of factors model: land, human, equipment and capital to any organizations in order to replace these production of factors and assist organizational development efficiently and effectively?System may be physical , like the solar system or an ecological system or which may be simply behavioral, like an organization. For example, a national economy may be a system, markets are systems, firms and factories are systems. Even, families and individuals are economic systems. The economy of the largest systems, national economy, may be called macroeconomy, which deals in terms of national aggregates for output, income, productivity. The economics of small systems, which are their parts or subsystems may be called microeconomics.

This is traditional production of factor model. for example, a system transforms inputs into outputs. An economic system is such a process. For example, factories are as systems take in raw materials, services etc. and change them into products for sale, i.e. output and consume them, thereby transforming them into rubbish, incidential is bad output. Also, countries consume their actural resources to enhance their standard of living and change them into waste products. If the system in question is national economy, some of the subsystems are might consider to be: the government, the firms, the consumers, the natural resources which it has at its disposal. Each subsystem is itself composed of subsystem of a lower order, such as a firm and each of these can be decomposed into further subsystems, depending on the purpose of the analysis. " All subsystems" interact need have individual characteistics, i.e. they are synergistic if they expected to raise producivity or efficiency or effectively. So, it needs high technological assistance to raise whose ability in economic view.

However, an economic system must continually adapt and restructure to meet the challenges of a changing economic environment if it is to prosper. For example, a firm must respond to its environment in the form of it customers' needs threats from its competitors, government regulations etc. Nowadays, technological innovation process and the nature of social economic and social changes which is occurring as the same time. So, organizations need to have strategic management to raise technological innovation to achieve raising productivity and efficiency aim. In the futue, (AI) robots will be possible one kind of new production of factor to assist organizational development and raise manufacturing efficiency and staffs' working performance in every team.

2 How does (AI) technological innovation occur in economic process?

What is economic process? It consists of the production and consumption of products and services by human. It is a process devised by human for own benefit pupose only. In the past, human lack advanced technological invention, e.g. family society required a much greater degree of organizational skill than hunting and gathering, it seems farming society does not need to achieve efficiency or productivity aim, because it is not industralized manufacturing society. Nowadays, the investment of resourcs is required for manufacturing processes for factories. The manufacturing stage thus needs machines, but it extends the economic process into the processing of manufacturing things, such as food. So, the knowledge and skills to do this are much more specialized again than farmer's or hunter's. So, technological innovation is needed to raise efficient productivity in factories, e.g. the increasing skills of manufacturing and the use of more intensive energy resources, such as coal and oil, gas, even solar energy either resources are from the sun or resources are from earth, e.g. fuels , heat, light, sound utilitiesm liquids , gases,solids. So, technological innovation is important to influence our economic development in our societies.

Economists usually classify what who call future of production into land, labor and capital. Why technological innovation is one another factor of production. For example, the economic process indicates that the first step is resources from the earth, e.g. solar energy supplies to earth to satisfy human needs. In the economic process, it needs these both supplies, driving force of transformation energy supply and captalyst , such as skills, knowledge, organization, creativity, creative participation in consumptions supply. Then, manufacturers shall change these both supplies to production and distribution of ordered materials and utilities in the economic process. Finally, it will provide to human consumption and human spent resources returned to earth in the final step. Another example of the elements of the economic process: the input is driving force of transformation stage of energy sources, e.g. sunlight firewood, oil and gas, coal , nuclear and household and industrial waste. Next is the economic process stage: facilitators, it includes tangible facilitator includes skills, knowledge, organization, creativity, e.g. language, science, technology, industry, machine, politics, law and order, defence, strategic plan, information systems, administration, tangible facilitator includes incentive system, e.g. money, banking, insurance, shares, private or public organizations, markets, land area. Finally, is the product of innovation stage, it includes utilities , such as electricity , heat, light, sound, motive power as well as ordered materials (products) , such as bread, meat, mine, shoes, clothes, houses, television, roads (public goods) etc. In future, (AI) robotic development will be possible participate to new economic process in order to raise global efficiency and performance for every businesses.

3 How (AI) robotic innovation information factor influences the product successful sale

What is the role of (AI) robotic innovation information (big data gathering method) ? Any markets requires product or service suppliers rationally act on the basic such information. But what who can't know in advance is how all the other participants are going to behave. The market clearing price would already be known. There would in fact be agreed prices and which everything could be exchanged, and there would be no market system at all. And so who come to market to settle the price/ quantity relationship. The theory is that which will arrive at a single price and quantity which reflect supply and demand. However, the number of interactions or pieces of information to be transmitted doubles with every new participants. However, the requirement for information is not limited to the particular market in question. A compromise between the number of people needed to make more nearly " perfect" in the economic sense, and the quantity of information needed to allow it to arrive at a unique price/ quantity relationship. The concept of degrees of freedom is widely used in different technological forms, e.g. engineering industry, the equipment is used by manufacturers to make pencils will be worn out to some extent in the process, and this forms an energy path straight to earth from the market in which the equipment was bought. Similarly wear and tear on the equipment used to make the intermediates and the raw materials will also form direct paths to earth from the markets in which were bought. It seems technological innovation factor of production can bring the pencil stationery product innovation when the new pencil stationey product is produced the more excellent quality by the new machines innovation.

In an economic system which is working " perfectly" according to the definitations, output is therefore a function of available energy and the technological skills to apply it to conversion of inputs into materials and utilities . In a market economy, given the availability of inputs of energy and materials, and the necessary information, the only factor which can bring this about in the long term is a change in the energy efficiency of its conversion process, i.e. the energy consumed unit of output of the same total production. This depends in the application of skills and design, that is technology factor of production.

Why (AI) big data gathering information can influence product sale ability. For example, the commodity is technologically complex like a computer, an aircraft or even a refrigetator. One is buying not just the piece of equipment, but also its specification because few people would understand the parts of the machine, let alone be able to judge their quality. Furthermore, one is also buying the future performance of the machine in operationm , its fuel consumptionm reliability, service costs, length of life, resistance to obsolescence etc. Probably the only guarantee that any information obtained on these points is valid is the reputation of the manufacturer.

Purchasers estimate chose chances of surviving the guarante period. Brand names are a way of simplisfying information flows. Such problems of defining the commodity and so handling the information necessary to arrive at a stable price, are magnified when counterfeit products, such as are flooding on to the market at present, find their way into markets for genuine products. Buyers will be unable to distinguish unless who are experts and sometimes that may need chemical analysis or destructive testing. This is a recent phenomenon to buy technological products.

4 Why does (AI) big data gathering information technology influence the real market system change ?

Can (AI) big data gathering information technology be one kind of production of factor to influence the real market system change to be more fast speed of market information communication in global industries? The market system in the real world includes: the first is manual work (manpower) element, in effect the provision of an elementary utility for consumption in a conversion process. If labors are not providing manpower, who become unemployed. Unemployment is not simply leaving a resource at a particular time, it is an injustice and a burden one the very real society which economics is supposed to help. Moreover, the unemployed can't spend the money who don't earn, and so buyers are reward from the economic process. The second is catalytic skills, knowledge, organization and creativity element which applied to the conversion processes which turn raw materials into products and utilities for consumption. In this case, who are as varied as the individuals that make up mankind, their accumulated knowledge, their capability of organising themselves to achieve their ends and not least their creativity,the ability to generate entirely new catalytic effects. Finally, is the incentive element, which is the prospect of participating in comsumption of the products of the economic process. The incentive system is cash for current or future exchange for products and utilities. The incentive system must be within the control of the social system of which it is a part. It can only be addressed by society as the whole system. However, for the individual and the firm too the creative must by definition come from outside and it is also depend on the rest of society.

What kinds of product can link between markets to increase speed of market information communication when global industries choose to apply (AI) big data gathering information technology to gather global competitors' product and client and price etc. business data. However, there are products which are linked in a different way by associated use. For products anyone who buys a vehicle must also be prepared to buy its fuel, tyres etc. A decision to buy the vehicle therefore automatically generates subsequent expenditure in the other markets. These markets are not so much competitors for buyers' money as complementary to each other. Sale in one must lead to sales in the other. This technological products have the same point, it is that which are needed to attempt to innovate their quality to raise their competitive ability to win their competitors. It seems that (AI) big data gathering information technological innovation can be a factor production to these different brands of vehicles and which related link products. Much the same occurs in technological industry. A company may feel that it is wise to buy related pieces of equipment from the same manufacturer, especially if they have to be connected in some way, whatever the price, within reason.

5 Can (AI) big data gathering timing of information influence real marketing system?

The analysis has shown that two sorts of (AI)big data gathering information are essential of the market is to reach " equilibrium" values of price and quantity: information concerns on the economic environment, which participants can obtain before the market opens; and information about the process of bargaining displayed, which can only be made available as the bargaining proceeds. However, buyers and sellers happen next. If the information acts as a reference point, it can only be a historical one. This is particularly so where markets operate continuously. There is always a lapse between the conclusion of deals and their display, so that new deals are always influenced to be not update information , in the absence of the most recent data, if dealing is busy. So, timing of information ought to be kept the most update to let buyers can have more confidence to make final choice to buy the broad of products. The quality of information which had to passed during bargaining in order to achieve on a unique price/quantity relationship increased rapidly with the number of participants because of the need of to allow everyone of buyers to interact with all the others.

It follows therefore, that as the number of participants becomes very large, the necessary information flows become much larger still and the time needed to allow this to take place increases greatly. So, timing of information can influence the participants would have changed or would have not changed their minds or gone home before proceedings could draw to a close. So, price and quality is the main message of information to influence consume individual attitude to decide to buy the product in market.

Timing of information can influence business cycles. It is well known that business activity is cyclinal. The short cycles of 4 to 5 years are best established , but consumers believe who can discern longer term and even very long term cycles of activity with periods of up to 50 years. Cyclical behavior, can only occur where these is an imperfect response to change, because of imperfect information. In general, this sort could not caused by the response time behavior of individual markets. Whatever the nature of the link, it is clearly the case that the price/quality relationship in individual markets is varying independently of the factors which might normally be expected to affect it in isolated systems. So, cyclical phenomena in business are strong evidence of the market process network behaving as a system.

In conclusion, markets are activites to exchange products and services. The elements of economic chains together to allow modern industrial economies or (AI) big data gathering information technological economy to function with all their complexity. They are essential to change and they permit innovation. However, markets are not well represented by the conventional supply/demand schedules, in particular because these can not include the effects of time as an variable factor. It is much clear to represent timing of information as systems in the form of flow diagrams showing the movement of products from innovative processes through markets to consume. Revenue from the market then supplies feedback to product manufacturers, and the whole system responds at different rates to different levels of feedback from clients. An effective medium of exchange is necessary for proper responses to be made. The complexity of the modern world, where price and quantity and quality in the market are all can't exist without the timing of information factor influence. Price signals are often confused by products, imperfect or incomprehensible information and the various effects of time, and in any case quantities to be supplied to the market have to be decided well in advance of market day. The whole trend a modern industrial economy or technological economy is towards product differentiation. Such as mobile phone, laptop computer etc. technologic products. Manufacturers often need to innovate design, quality, functions to adapt to client's individual need. So, technological innovation is often a production of factors to invent high technological products. Services too can't be fitted into price/quantity schedules because it is impossible to define the product. Otherwise, the categorisation of human as labor, having a price/quantity relationship, when who are clearly , each is an individual learning system, changing every day of whose life and changing the economic process accordingly. In fact, human must necessarily be accepted as a feature of modern life, to protect to let them to enjoy high quality of life. So, individual economic stage will be needed to enter technological economic stage in economic environment. Indeed by limiting the rate of change such actions may in no small measure be a condition of stability for the people in an economy . It seems that (AI) big data gathering information technological innovation is one factor of production and it has close relstionship to timing of reasonable price and quality information to persuade consumers to choose to buy the manufacturer's product.

6 (AI) big data gathering information can reduce the cost basis of economic activity to any businesses

(AI) big data gathering information technology can help any organizations to reduce the time and human effort economic cost. In conversion processes there is always some wear and tear of the fixed asset, the equipment, building etc. which reduce their capacity to produce in future. Of course after the money has been spent on the plant, it is no longer cost of operating. This is not technological obsolescence which results from development of better ways of meeting market needs. The efficiency of produrers is continually improved and the most effective use of the resources available is continually improved and the most effective use of the resources available to the society, and the most effective use of the resources available to the society is made according to the criteria of economic values. The under-utilised resources locked up in the inefficient operation are not necessarily lost. The producer may learn in time to use them better. So that who can eventually compete on moral equal terms, or who may give way to another who knows how to manage the resources more efficiently. If however, the inefficiency has a deep-rooted cause which can not be remedied, or even a producer who is capable of improvement but refuses to act, then the resources run down to extiaction faster than ordinary wear and tear would cause them to. So, it suppose to technological innovation can help producers to reduce cost for long term. It is cost benefit to producers for long term.

For agricultural industry example, it was said that the only way for a farmer to increase whose not revenue significantly, once who was farming as efficiently as possible, was to increase the area of land under cultivation. But technological innovation is such production of factor, it might be a case for increasing the area under cultivation in order to make better use of a piece of equipment, such as a tractor, and so spread its cost over more production. Another might be in the processing industries, such as petrochemicals or oil where many new producers with the same global threats and opportunities. The input costs when products or utilities move in the direction of time and energy in the economic process. If one opportunity for using the resources is selected, then another potential use will be foregone. Opportunity costs are therefore distinguished from input costs by time. So, the production for factor of technological innovation can be opportunity cost, if the manufacturer felt who can spend less manufacturing expenditure for long term. Due to who lose to use money to spend other expenditure or invest, who choose to invent technological innovation to reduce long term input costs. The best opportunities are those which maximise prices and minimise costs. SO, (AI) big data gathering technology can be applied to argicultural industry to help farmers to reduce farming time and farming equipment cost to grow any fruit, vegetable and rise , tomotato , potato etc. food in production of factor view.

Producers try to achieve higher market prices by giving their products some distinguishing feature which whose hope will attract buyers away from other competitors and /or generate new buyers, what marketers call product differentiation. In effect they try to move their product into a new market, perhaps thought of as " up market" or a " market niche", but certainly in separate market for analytical purpose. Even if they can not do this, which is unusual in these days of increasing technological innovation and communication , operators continually try to improve their processes in order to reduce costs. If always requires the investment of new resources, e.g. technological innovation.

In the real world, it is not possible to differentiate products or processes except in time. The overall result is to move the process in the direction of economic improvements, in effect the behavior of economic system as a learning system. Time introduces all the risks and opportunities which present themselves to the processor. In the analysis which follows , we classify and illustrate the various aspects of economy of scope under the traditional economic heading of labor, capital, and land. Energy and information, technological innovation are considered too ,because which are fundamental to all systems and process in economic activity.

7 The (AI) big data gathering technological innovation benefits

First, (AI) big data gathering technological innovation can bring to help organizations to reduce staff number and divide labor to raise different department work efficiency and performance benefits. For the division of labor benefits example. This is a complex process into stages in which a worker can specialize, thus allowing who to perform that particular task more efficiently, i.e. at lower cost per unit of effective output than if who had to undertake the whole process. Such an improvement in efficiency results from the more effective learning, greater development of skills and more intensive application over a period of time which becomes possible when a task is easily within the capacity of one person.

It is easily confused with advances in (AI) big data gathering technology, capital investment or scale of operation. Division of complex process into stages may subsequently allow the development of specialised technologies for the individual stages, and this may result in specialised equipment, and hence capital investment . Similiarly, if the process is carried out with less labor and/or lower raw material costs for each unit of output, those concerned may in principle decide either the produce more . Output or the produce the same output with less input. It seems technological innovation can bring low cost benefits. In fact, new technology imposes a diseconomy on the old, eg. functions using old technology are at a cost disadvantage and must adopt or eventually disappear under free competition. So, new technology is the source of growth and adoptation in economy. The solutions to a diseconomy of scape lies in a change of scope, for example, in this case different establishments operating at different times, and perhaps with different prices. If capital investment are differentiated be improved to give longer life and better use, which in effect reduces their cost in use. For example, continuing advantages in technology allow processes to be designed in such a way that which deliver the same output with ever decreasing inputs of materials, labor or energy. Thus waste is minimised by planning and the conservation of process energy, and maintenance is reduced by change of design or the use of new materials. It may often worth spending more on equipment initially to reduce those time dependent costs. This sort of efficiency is the most obvious effect of scope rather than scale.

Deterioration and obsolescence means wear and tear are the changes which occur in artefacts as which are used , i.e. deterioration , or changes in quality or scope with time. These are not simply time effects because which depend both on the original design and on the conditions of use, such as maintenance skills and even simple care and attention. Obsolescence is difference to depreciation, it relates to the battle in the market place . The networks of markets brings products and therefore all conversion processes into competition for the same revenues. Old products will be not popular because which become harder to sell. Obsolescence, therefore depends not only on time, but also on competition, in the same time of business. It seems technological innovation can avoid obsolescence occurrence to old products to raise which competitive ability to the same markets. However, there was hardly an element in the competitive cost structures of conversion processes which was not disturbed in a way which differentiated country form country, industry from industry and firm from firm, such as (AI) big data technological innovation to any old products, which production of factor cost structures is the same basically.

8 What is the relationship between the process of (AI) big data gathering technological innovation and the production of factor?

The term "innovation" is used to describe the deliberate process by which a new product or process comes to be sold in the market. Technology innovation can be applied to conversion processes, which requires the use of energy, or their products, which have an economic energy content. It is therefore a function of all the forces which shape markets: manufacturing, processing, technology, buying, selling, information, prices costs etc. So an innovating organization may be a whole company or it may be an individual. Other forms of innovation (production of factor) relate to the sale of services within what defines as the facilitiation system. That sort of exchange is not specifically considered to be one production of factor, because it involves different adoptation processes and response times, and doesn't of itself add to the quantity of products or utilities sold.

However, invention can not be defined to one production of factor and it is to be distinguished to innovation. We can describe invention is as the process of discovering something completely new, i.e. a new fact or relationship. It is an important scientific advance. Invention enlarges the scope of man's awareness, but it doesn't necessarily have direct economic value in itself. If it is sold, it is the sale of an idea, an exchange of a little creativity for an incentive within the facilities system. It isn't marketed as a new product of a conversion process. No energy of conversion is involved. The great majority of inventions do not enter into the economic process and which do not become innovations until that happens.

If the change of scope results in a new (AI) manufacturing technological process for making a product or utility which is already being sold, this can't be differentiated from the existing product or utility in the market concerned. To be successful the new process must make it at lower unit cost than existing process. The result then is that either the price of the product fulls and processes to improve are imposed to competition or more net revenue is accumulated. So the aims of the factors of technological innovation production include: The introduction of a process for making at a lower unit cost a non-differentiated product which is sold into a commodity market, and the development and sale of a differentiated product which will draw buyers away from other markets, or draw money into the market which would not otherwise have been spent.

The nature of (AI) manufacturing technological innovation how causes factor of production. The process of technological innovation is the arrangement of materials at the elementary, say atomic or molecular level, or of components or the design of new machines, or of the relative positions of components, for example, the location of nodes in networks. There are the three levels at which the scope of the economic process may be changed. However, technological innovation can't seem without some change in the way materials ae ordered. It follows that all technological innovation flows initially from some change in a conversion process. Thus technological in the result of investment in conversion processes, where investment is defined as laying down fixed assets and so it requires a change in the use of energy consumed during conversion to make useful products. The flexible manufacturing system themselves are examples of the third level of innovation, the spatial arrangement of components and hence the link between them. Patterns of communication have changed and are continue to change as a result of new technoloby in the use of energy and the convergence of computer, data maipulation and telecommunication. Flexible manfacturing systems manufacture components in rather than having them made by supplies industries and transported to an assembly plant in batches. The new arrangements reduce both the time of reponse to market changes and all the skills of components which are needed to give flexibility of response in conventional systems , i.e. they give economy of scope.

9 How to response times in (AI) manufacturing technological innovation?

In the terminology which have developed above, the behavioral effects may be considered as adjustment of the scope of the sellers and buyers organizations as the process of acceptance of the innovation in the market proceed. Costs and risks in technological innovation, innovation requires the commitment of resources over a long period, and it is therefore subject to the same kind of risks as any investment in conversion processes. The most obvious risk is that the technological difficulties are in the initial concept, with the result that no returns will be earned and the resources sunk in the investment may have been wasted. There is a set of market-related reasons why technological success may not result in an innovation. By the time, the new process or product is ready for the market, the demand for it may have receded or may never have materialised. This may be the result of fulfiment of the potential users‘ needs by another technology, i.e. the innovation may be technologically obsolete before it may be because of a change of fashion or styles of living.

Two conclusions may be drawn, firstly, the product manufacturer has a good foresight and understanding is needed when undertaking projects which consume large amount of capital, or it may result in gross waste, because the future is always uncertain, however, the analysis, secondly, there is a limit to the rate of constructive innovation in an economic system, the ratio at which the system can accumulate. Hence, some product manufacturer will feel the technological innovation can be a good production of factor , such as a cost advantage is termed a competitive advantages. It is a broader term than the comparative advantages of traditional economy because of does not depend on a favorable climate or an abundance of natural resource. It is developed and maintained entirely by the skills of the people in the firms which are involved.

Technology is like on the economic process, because once knowledge about transforming inputs into outputs has been obtained, and especially after it has been implemented, it doesn't disappear. Technological innovation moves the whole process. Thus, economy of scope confer permanent advantages on those who have them. Economy of scope is to be obtained from all the elements of the economic process which change with time and these are suspectible to improvement, whether as separate elements. They involve people, and their capacity to learn and improve, and material in all their different forms.

10 Why technological innovation will be one factor of production to technological manufacture industry.

Innovation is the process by which new products' processes methods or services are created. Innovation offers added value for and users by providing better and/or cheaper functionality than previous options. Innovation combines changes in technology, business models, organization etc. The basic idea may be a new technical solutions, a new business model or a change in organization. In a competitive economy, no business can survive long term without updating its products and services or the ways in which are produced or delivered. Innovation policy must promote renewal across all business sectors and not just focus on high technological industries.

Since most innovations are complex and each subsystem has its own limitation , an important part of the innovation process is finding the right balance between conflicting demands. In most cases, there are several possible ways of providing a new function to users, or possible applications of a new technology. Which combination of features the market will prefer can't be predicted with any certainty. Whether the origin was a market opportunity on a new technological capability to one part of the production of factor to the product.

Innovation integrates knowledge from a number of different fields: technology, marketing, design, economic etc. In the production of factor view, it is hard to collect all the necessary competences in a single organization. Because technological products need to be updatd to keep competition in market. Thus, innovation has become a process of constant with suppliers and competitors, with consultants and with academic researchers. In the production of factor view, the capacity to innovate depends on how well different parts of this system are adapted to each other and how well they work together.

Today, the relationship between science and innovation is more complex and interdependent. Science-based technologies, such as microelectronics or biotechnology could not have been developed without scientific understanding, but modern science is equally dependent on advanced technology. Economists tend to prefer technology performance standards, but these risk favouring marginal improvements to existing technologies when discouraging more radical, long term solution. Also, economists tend to think of innovation as a production processes. A more production describes innovations as an experimental learning proces in which organizations and individuals build new competence. This term "research-based competence" is rather than " science-based knowledge or "scientific information".

I shall argue that economists' active process is a better way of think about the relationship between industry and academic research. Whether can the production of factor of technological innovation make use of the tools and results of research in addressing real world problem to manufacture any technological products? This main concern at the time was whether research and innovation were essentially different activities which should be supported in different ways or whether it was important to deal with both aspects together since which were interdependent. However, innovation is a process of searching, experimenting and learning. Consumers can learn about how new products, processes and services are created, how firms build competence for this and what information sources which use. So, I feel technological innovation ought be one part of production process or production of factor to some manufacturers. Such as, searching is needed for better ways of doing worth which things. Experimenting is needed because consumers can't seen in advance the best way of accomplishing a desired outcome or indeed what users really want or need. Learning is needed because actors involved in an innovation process will learn from it. The kind of learning which changes consumers' ability to solve future challenges and opportunities. However, economists often think of innovation is as a production prcocess, where knowledge transformed into a new product. We measure research and development investment, relating these to outcomes in the form of patents, new products and productivity or economic growth. Innovations are not just new technological products or processes, it also mentions organizational innovations, new distribution channels, new business models etc. In fact, it is often misleading to think about technical or organizational innovation as separate processes. Most innovations combine changes in technology, business models organization etc. in production process.

What kinds of product can belong to high technological manufacturing. For example, the world's most advanced steel plants and paper mills can never be classified as high technology because of their complementary need for high levels of investment in fixed capital, and aerospace manufacture is classified as medium technology. The standard definition of high technology measures research and development intensity not the generation or use of advanced technology as such. A far better measure is the proportion of scientists, engineers and highly qualified technicians in the labor force. For computer industry example, innovations in the field of rabotic manufacturing, nanotechnologies and human genetics research all have been enabled by low cost computational and control capabilities supplied by computers and software. Reducing the cost of software important objectives of the U.S. software industry. However, the complexity of the software industry to support the U.S. is computerized economy is increasing at an alarming rate. Software nonperformance and failure are expensive. In actuality many factors contribute to the quality issues facing the software industry. These include marketing strategies, limited liability by software vendors, and decreasing returns to testing.

At the core of these issues is the difficulty in defining and measuring software reliability, usability, efficiency, maintenability and portability. Information problems are further complicated by the fact that even with substantial testing, software developers don't truly know how their products with perform until who encounter real scenarios. The similiar industries with need have technological innovation in the productive process (production of factor), such as automotive and aerospace equipment manufacturers and related electronic communications equipment manufacturers. Quality is defined as attribute factor to different kinds of software product. Defining the attributes of software quality and determining the metrics to access the relative value of each attribute are not formalized processes. Because users place different values on each attribute depending on the product's use, it is important that quality attributes be observable to consumers. The technological innovation is one production of factor to software industry. Due to software attributes have those accurateness, interoperability, security, reliability (maturity, recoverability); usability (understandability, learnability, operability); efficiency (time behavior, resource behavior); maintainability (analyzability, changeability, stability, testability); portability (abaptability, installability, replaceability). It seems that due to software attribute have these characteristics, so it causes technological innovation is one production of factor to software industry.

Nowadays, human needs have been increasing, external factor can influence some industries cause technological innovation is one production of factor need. Together, these tends are going to reshape now human live and work, reorganize our social, economic and political institutions and redistribute power and reward in society. In the longer term, as machine learning and computer power intelligence technological innovation needs from consciousness, as machine learning and computer from consciousness, as improving health technologies allow for biological enhancements and species divergence, and as the final frontier is also needed by space travel, technological and social transformation will increasingly change what is means to be human. However, human have to better understand how our world is changing and by what forces those changes are driven . So, because human have high living quality needs, so it causes many new products have technological innovation to manufacture new product or to raise high quality need to satisfy our daily life. It will cause of factor to some products.

The (AI) manufacturing technological innovation factor can influence the economic of the pork meat production in agricultural industry. For example, the economy of the pork meat production on a farm has been carried out with the help of the method of production functions (factor-product and factor-factor). The influence of the weight of an animal on the daily growth tells us that the growth is increased with the increse of the entry weight to 19kg and with the exit weight of the fattened animal of 100 kg. So, the relationship between the daily growth and the feed costs by a feeding day shows us the tendency of than increase of a daily growth with the increase of the feed costs, e.g. with the increase of labor inputs to 2.6 hours/100 kg of the live weight and the increased profit to 29 monetary units. Labor productivity grows with the increase of the capacity usage to 87% and then it decrease. The economy of agricultural production considerably depends on the development of cattle-breeding as a natural capacity of transforming plant products into high quality cattle products. Cattle-raising production influences the food quality, the development of food production industry, the output of high quality and healthy safe product and the development of agricultural economy. So, it seems technological innovation can be a production of factor to influence farm agricultural industry to assist farmers to apply high, e.g. agricultural technology (skills) produces high quality and tastic of farming met to satisfy consumers' diet needs.

Growth of total factor productivity (TFP) can provide society with an opportunity to increase the welfare of people. In particular, in the simplest framework, change in labor productivity factor depends on change (TFP) and capital deepening. How to change TFP? I shall suppose the technological innovation method is a factor to reduce labor cost, but it can raise labor productivity and products or goods of quality to satisfy consumers' needs in competitive market. Economists often define the knowledge economy as production and services based on knowledge-intensive activities tht contribute to an accelerated pace of technical and scientific technology, as well as rapid absolescence. Knowledge is now recognized as the driver of productivity and economic growth, leading to a new focus on the role of information, technology and learning in economic performance. In the knowledge-based economy, innovation is driven by the interaction of producers and users in the exchange of both codified and tacit knowledge: This interactive model has replaced the traditional linear model of innovation. The knowledge-intensive and high technology, economy tends to be the most dynamic in terms of output and employment growth. Changes in technology and particularly the advent of information technologies are making educated and skilled labor more valuable, and unskilled labor less. So, the technological innovation production of factor will bring skilled labor needs, more and unskilled labor needs less.

Although, it can maximize the benefits of technology for productivity, but it can raise unemployment number of non-skillful labor, because the high technological product firms will choose to dismiss the non-skillful labor and will employ skillful labor when innovation which decide to apply technological innovation method to produce whose products. For example, output and employment are expanding fastest in high technology industries, such as computers, electronic and aerospace. Also, knowledge-intensive service sectors, such as online education, communication and information(long distance call) are growing even faster, such as internet shopping technological business can be production of factor to let universities can teach students from internet, such as distance learning. Internet can be used to adventise and sell products from businessman individual website more easily. Also, mobile can use internet to do same benefits, such as laptop or desktop kinds of high technological computer products. It seems technological benefits can attract consumer individual consumption more easily. So, skillful biased technical change is a shift in the production technology that favors skilled over unskilled labor by increasing its relative productivity and therefore, its relative demand. In fact, skill-biased technical change is a shift in the production technology (factor of production that favors skilled, e.g. more relative productivity) and therefore, its relative demand.

11 How can external and internal factors affect the product and (AI) manufacturing process innovation?

In fact, the competition advantages of a company strongly depends on its possibility to benefit from innovational activities. Understanding the factors how which affect product and process innovation and their effort is necessary to be proved why innovational activities can be the one part production of factors to some new products. It has close relationship between product and business processes innovation and industry maturity and customer needs (demand) technological opportunities and investment attractiveness and company size and export orientation. These external and internal factors can influence innovational activities to some new products.

Nowadays, fast technology development, combined with the globalization and fast changes in with the globalization and fast changes in customer demand, implies that a competitive advantage of a company. So, companies will spans great effort in beating the competition innovations have a vital influence on economic development of a country. On the macro level, innovations have a vital influence on economic development that innovations are more and more present both a developed and developing countries that wish to grow developing countries that wish to grow fast and become developed. If we simply categorize companies all innovative or non-innovative. Among different innovation's categorizations is developed by researchers, the most important are: classification according to the type of innovation to degree of innovativity, innovations can be classified as incremental, semi-radical and radical innovations (Davila et al 2006), who indicates that radical innovations potentially offer huge profits and competitive advantage, but demand considerably high risk level, much company effort need and resource engagement. Otherwise, incremental innovations have more modest returns, but demand lower risk level, level of efforts and resources and are generally more successful. Finally, semi-radical innovations are somewhere between the two of them.

According to (Christensen 2003) explained to an innovations can be sustaining and disruptive. Sustaining innovations can be placed in the whole range from incremental to radical and discuptive are either semi-radical or radical. Sustaining innovations are those that improve existing products or process, disregarding the degree of improvement. Disruptive innovations create a huge growth offering a new of performances which has even it is inferior from the start comparing to existing technologies' performances a potential to become superior. Companies are advised to accept what is the best for their situation and design innovational processes, develop aptitudes, allocate resources and form partnerships in compliance to that decision.

In fact, many external and internal factors can affect companies chose product innovations, because process, innovations or their combination, e.g. factors include industry maturity, customer needs and expectations , technological opportunities, investment attractiveness, intensity of cmpetition, company size, origin of ownership and export orientation. In the industry maturity stage, as a market matures and customer needs become defined in a better way, companies transfer the focus of their competition to expenses and economy of range investing more in business processes in order to make them more effective and more efficient. Customer needs and expectations are essential for process innovations that improve process effectiveness. Orientation to customers and their satisfaction are well-known concept in the field of a total quality management.

The point of view that market demand presents the main determine the rate and activities of an invention because each rational company that tends to make profit is responsive to economic stimuli . According to Schmookler (1962) demand growth is prior to the growth in innovative activites, i.e. market requests guarantee stimuli for companies to innovate and take up new technologies. This concept is popularly called " market pull" in a sense that a market pulls innovations.

12 What is (AI) production of factor knowledge economy ?

I shall give evidences to explain why technological innovation can be one kind of production factor to some technological product manufacture industry nowadays. Nowadays, we are entering the knowledge based economy stage. Knowledge is now recognized as the driver of productivity and economic growth, leading to new focus or the role of information technology and learning in economic performance. The knowledge based economy and its relationship is as traditional economics, as reflected in " new growth theory". Because every technological product manufacturer needs workers to acquire a range of skills and to continuously adapt these skills underlines the " learning economy". The importance of knowledge and technology diffusion requires better understanding of knowledge networks and " national innovation systems".

Firstly, knowledge-based economies which are directly based on the production, distribution and use of knowledge and information. The is reflected in the trend in growth in high technology investment, high technological industries, move highly-skilled labor and associated productivity gains. Also required is tacit knowledge including the skills to use and adapt codified knowledge-based economy, innovation is driven by the interaction of producers and users in the exchange of both codified and tacit knowledge.

Employment in the knowledge-based economy is characterized by increasing demand for more highly skilled workers. The knowledge-intensive and high-technology tend to be the most dynamic in terms of output and employment growth. The science system, essentially public research laboratories and institutes of highest education, carries out key functions in the knowledge-based economy, including knowledge production, innovative technology. So, the traditional functions of producing new knowledge through basic research and educating new generations of scientists and engineers with its newer role of collaborating with industry in the transfer of knowledge and technology. For example, our societies tend to research institutes and academic increasingly have industrial partners for financial as well as innovative purposes, but most combines this with their essential role in more generic research and education.

In general, our understanding of what is happening in the knowledge-based economy is constrained by the extent and quality of the available knowledge-rated indicators. So, available knowledge-rated indicated. So, development of indicators of the knowledge-based economy must start with improvements to more traditional input indicators of research and development expenditures and research personal. Better in indicators are also needed of knowledge stocks and flows, particularly relating to the diffusion of information technologies, in both manufacturing and service sectors; social and privates rates of return to knowledge investments to the impact of innovation technology in productivity and growth.

However, knowledge is such as human being (human capital) and in innovative technology has always been central to economic development. When human is entering the 21 ST century, our output and employment are expanding tastes in high technology industries, such as computers, electronics and aerospace investment is thus being directed to high-technology products and services, particularly information and communicating technologies. Computers and related equipment are the fastest growing component of tangible investment. Equally important are more intangible investments in research and development, the training of the labor force, computer software and technical expertise. Hence, it causes employment is growing in high technology, science-based sectors ranging from computers to pharmaceuticals. Also, research and development causes manufacturing sector is losing jobs. Due to those jobs are more highly skilled and pay higher wages than those in lower technology sectors (e.g. textiles and food processing). Knowledge-based jobs in service sectors are also growing strongly. Indeed, non-production or knowledge workers those who don't engage in the output of physical products, are the employees in most demand in a wide range of activities from computer technicians, through physical therapists to marketing specialists.

Economists continue to search for the foundations of economic growth. Traditional, " production functions" focus on labor, capital , materials and energy, land; however, knowledge and technology are external influence on production. Analytical approaches are being developed. So, that knowledge can be included more directly in production functions. Investment in knowledge can raise productive capacity of the other factors of production as well as transform them into new products and processes from innovative technology.

According to the neo-classical production function, returns diminish is as more capital is added to the economy an effect which may be offset, however, by the flow of new technology. In new growth theory, knowledge can raise the returns on investment, which can contribution to the accumulation of knowledge. Technological change can also raise the relative marginal productivity of capital through education and training of the labor force, investment in research and development and the creation of new managerial structures and worth organization. In fact, incorporating knowledge into standard economic production functions is not easy task, as this factor defies some fundamental economic principles, such as that of scarcity, knowledge is intangible, but labor, capital, land, equipment etc. production of factors which can be tangible or measured. However, some kinds of knowledge can be easily reproduced and distributed at lower cost to abroad set of users, which tends to undermine private ownership. Knowledge is a much broader concept than information, which is generally the " know-what", and "know-why" components of knowledge. There are also the types of knowledge which come closet to being market commodities or economic resources to be fitted into economic production functions.

Knowledge can divide know-why and know-how both kinds of concept. Know-why means to scientific knowledge of the principles and laws of nature. This kind of knowledge underlines technological development and product and process advances in most industries. The production and reproduction of know-why is often organized in specialized organizations, such as research-laboratories and universities. Otherwise, know-how means to skills or the capability to do something. Business judging market prospects for a new product or a personnel manager selecting and training staff have to use their know-how. The same is true for the skilled worker operating complicated machine tools. Finally, knowledge-who becomes increasingly important. Know-who involves information about who knows what and who know how to do what. It involves the make if possible to get access to experts and use their knowledge efficiently. So, knowledge economy brings those conditions to our societies. One hypothesis is that globalization and international competition have led to decrease relative demand for less-skilled workers of the phenomenon; an alterative explanation is that innovative technology change has become more strongly biased in favor of skilled workers, changes in firm behavior is as the main reason for falling real wages for low-skilled workers. Thus, innovative technology and knowledge economy has close relationship to cause knowledge workers can bring high technological products of production of factor in technological product manufacture industry.

13 (AI) Production of factor internal technical skill

Secondly, it is the internal skill biased technical change influences. Skill-biased technical change is a shift in the production technology, that flavors skilled over unskilled labor by increasing its relative productivity and , therefore, its relative demand of innovative technology of production factor. The direction of technical changes i.e. whether new capital complements skilled or unskilled labor may be determined by innovators' economic incentives shaped by relative prices, the size of the market and institutions.

Economic theory views the production technology as a function describing that a collection of factor inputs can be transformed into output, and it defines technical change as a shift in the production of function. In fact, given who observed movements of the production function only concentrates on , such as land supply, labor numbers, equipment supply, capital demand factors. Therefore,To make sense of these recent developments, the concept of factor biased technical change can be another production of factor to influence the new technical products quantities change. For example, the timing of the rise in the skill premium has changed the rapid diffusion of information and communication technologies in the workplace environment in any high technological industry generally nowadays. For example, expenditures in information processing equipment and software, is as a share of U.S. private non-residential fixed investment, rose from 6% in 1960 year to 40% in 2000 year. At the heart of those dynamic change.

This is an improvement in the quality and productivity of all those equipment products, relying heavily on semiconductors like computers, software and switching equipment underlying much of communication technology. In the early adoption phase of a new technology, that those who adapt more quickly can reap some benefits. As time goes by, there will be enough makers learning how to work with the new technology to offset the wage differential. Note the difference with the hypothesis set, where the effect of capital deepening on the skill premium is permanent. Also, information technologies production of factor can reduce costs of data storage, communication, monitoring and supervision activities within the firm which causes a shift towards a new organizational design. In particular, the layers in the hierarchical structure can be reduced, so that the organization of the firm becomes "flatter". So, workers no longer perform routinized, responsible for a wide range of tasks within teams. Therefore, adaptable workers verses at multi-tasking activities benefits is a factor of production to reduce internal cost of any firms.

Due to technological innovation causes the layers in the hierarchical structure can be reduced, so that the organization of the firm becomes "flatter". How technological innovation can influence internal skill biased technical change to orgnizational structure. Development behavioral means it is through managment theory. So, high technological skillful organization will choose to apply theory x more than theory y because this technological innovation will reduce some unskillful staffs and give more effort and duties to those skillful staffs to use high technological skill to do whose jobs daily and who will feel lazy and unhappy to do extra more technological jobs. Theory x assumptions are the average human being dislike of work and work avoid if who can, most people must be controlled, directed or threatened with punishment to adequate effort to action organization objective; otherwise, theory y assumptions are people like to use physical and mental effort to work as natural as play and rest, human being dislike work, a source of satisfaction, threat of punishment are not being effort. Hence, technological innovation can cause organizations to change whose structure and skill staffs need to do more jobs. It causes employer need to give extristic and intrinsic motivations to satisfy whose skillful staffs needs to raise efficiency, e.g. giving more tangible reward, as salary, benefit, security, promotion, good contract of condition of work service, comfortable workplace environment as well as using one ability to achieve who feel apprecation, positive being treating of psychological satisfactory needs.

In technological innovation of organization structure, the management committee needs to concern whose skillful technological labor individual psychological needs. Because technological innovation is one important production of factor and it has close relationship between motivation and staff individual efficiency and productivity. As Maslow's hierarchy of needs indicates people (staffs) mean having satisfied to achieve motivation behavior, the lowest love is basic physiological, the need for food, as salary, safe working condition, then is job security, benefit. Next is friendship at work group, after is promotion, payment increasing, high status of job title. Finally is achievement in work advancement opportunitie creative task in related aspect at work motivation. Hence, after the traditional non-technological innoviation of organization changed the technological innovation of organizational structure, management needs to concern that motivation is needed to develop of behavioral through contributed to management theory. Every organiztion manageer needs to know what its team staffs whose indvidual needs, it includes extrinsic needs, e.g. salary, promotion, security as well as intrinsic needs, e.g. achievement, appreciaton. If the employees feel extrinsic needs are more than intrinsic needs, the managers can consider what extrinsic needs, the managers can consider what extrinsic needs of whose employee individual need. If the employee feels intrinsic needs are more than extrinsic needs, the manage can consider what intrinsic needs the employee individual actual need in order to motivate the skillful worker to work efficiently and raising productivity.

After changing the technological innovation of organizational structure, the management needs to concern how to plan to raise its productivity from its production of factor of technological innovation. Planning is looking ahead, control is looking back, every organization must need strategic plan, operative plan and tastic plan for every department to give aim for its mission objectives. Then it needs to achieve its any short term plans or long term plans efficiently, e.g. how to achieve to produce and to sell 5,000 computers sale objective or how to increase to achieve 20% profit or productivity objective from 10% within one year. So, after the technological innovation production of factor influences the organization needs to find reasons what how to influence it can not achieve these new objectives within one year. Then, it needs to find reasons and revises to solve challenges to control it can achieve it's planning objectives. For example, SWOT method indicates what its internal strengths and weaknesses, external threats and opportunities are. To aim achieve its planning strategic plan every year. Before the organization is not technological innovation, it can't have control is looking ahead, due to planning is looking back because organization can;t know what it's mission and objectives can't achieve to revise if it has no any strategic plan, operational plan and tactical plan for top, middle and low level to let different department managers to know what it's mission and objectives are planned to achieve before the organization has not changed the technological innovation of organizational structure in the year. Besides, after the technological innovation changed the organizational structure. The management needs to concern how to implement it's strategies effectively. The technological innovation of organization needs to change its old long term strategic plan to be new long term strategic plan in the top level, e.g. one year what is its new mission for its technologcial innovation, e.g. Apple brand of computer company needs to innovate its old style computer design to know how to adapt the young client group needs (demand) in this competitive computer technological product industry.

Finally, after innovative organizational structure, mangement needs to concern how to raise skillful labor individual productivity and efficiency, due to who need to increase more effort to do their jobs after technological innovation. I shall indicate on job training method. The advantages on limitations of different approaches to on the job training include the company needs to spend extra time and resources to train staffs or workers to work, when who are on the regular work time. Hence, it will lose staffs to do regular job duties, due who needs to learn how to do their job. So the employer needs to pay higher salary to every job trainer for long term if it needs to train many skillful labor after technological innovation. It can't ensure whether the training employees can work efficiently and know who are not the right staffs to get training. Hence, it will employ the staffs who are not right staffs to accept job training riskly if the mangement have not evaluate who have effort to be train to raise whose productivity and testing personal effort of evaluation is more important to the job trainers.

14 What are the (AI) technical change as exogenous or endogenous production of factor?

Finally, I shall indicate what the change is as exogenous or endogenous factor in the (AI) production function model to cause innovative technology to produce new technological product in manufacture industry. Although, economic theory firstly treated technology change is as a residual, the unexplained part remaining after the contribution of an increased quantity and quality of capital, labor and natural resources in output growth have been accounted for. However, the theory of economic growth reconsidered recently the nature of technological change and the concept of knowledge. Therefore, the new growth economic theory includes research and development is as a factor of influence in the macroeconomic models.

The endogenous or exogenous nature of technological change refers to its source: endogenous is internal to the national economy, being created by domestic private or public enterprise, when exogenous change is external originating from foreign sources. So, it seems research and development workforce is as new factor in the production function model. Although, technological progress, managerial improvements and innovation in general are nowadays largely regarded as key contributors to economic growth. Schumpeter (1939) defines technical progress in terms of production function, which describes the way the production output varies according to the quantity and quality of the input factors. So, the technological change represents the factor that shifts the production function.

From the theoretical viewpoint, it has difficult to separate knowledge from the other factors of the production function. The total labor factor productivity is usually estimated by output the capital and labor factors, weighted by their specific shares. Under perfect competition, the price of the production factors is equal to their marginal productivity, hence, their shares in outputs are equal to their exponents from the production function.

Otherwise, from the empirical point of view, there are difficulties of measurement, especially in the case of value added and research-development variables. So, from all available data on research and development input and outputs, research and development expenditures are most frequently used, along with the number of patents, the technological balance of payments, machinery and tools inputs etc. costs to measure of input in innovation.

Furthermore, the exponents of the new growth theory indicates modeled knowledge is as an output quality of the research and development sector and proved that contrary to the neoclassical conclusions of the diminishing-returns technology, the introduction of the human capital changes the production function into one with increasing returns. Thus, it seems total research and development expenditures are used in this model as a measure of total investments (material and intangible) in the research and development sector. However, in many studies, the research and development stock is calculated as the accumulated value of research and development expenditure after depreciation, a procedure which implies the assumption that all of the research and development expenditure certainly and that it's stock depreciates with a certain fixed rate. Since, long time-series data on R & D are rarely available, other studies assume that the growth rate of R & D expenditure to R & D stock is stable. Hence in innovation technological industry, the labor production factor can be divided into two components total employees population outside the research development sector and the number of employees in research and development. The same types of division was applied to the capital production factor.

Reference

Christensen, C.M. (2003) " the innovator's dilema", Harpercollins, New York.

Davila, T., Epstein, M. J., Shelton.R. (2006) " Making innovation work: How to manage it, measure it and profit from it". Warton school publishing, New Jersey.

Schmookler, J., (1962) " Economic sources of incentive activity, " the journal of economic history. vol. 22
, no. 1 (Mar. 1962), 1-20.

Schumpeter, J., A. (1939), business cycles: A Theoretical Historical And Statistical Analysis Of Capitalist Processes, New York: Macmillan.

Reference

Future of jobs survey, World Economic Forum.

Hauser, J. Tellis, G. J; Griffin, A. 2006. Research On Innovation: A Review And Agenda For Marketing Science. 25(6): 687-717.

J.P. Holdren & P.R. Enrlich, " Human population and the global environment", American Scientist, vol. 62 (1974), pp.282-92.

Joel E. Cohen, How many people can the earth support? (New York: Norton, 1995), pp. 212-36, 261-62.

Mohr, G. J. Griffin, A. 2010. Research On Innovation : A Review And Agenda For Marketing Science. 25 (6): 687-717.

Names of drivers have abbreviated to ensure legibility. Future of jobs survey, World Economic Forum.

" Presence to prosperity", PWC Growth Markets Centre Report: http://www.pwc.com/gx/en/growth-markets-centre/presence-to-profitability.jhtml

CHAPTER V

Non-manual driving public transport tools innovation

Why MTR underground train transportation needs to know passenger behaviour

Understanding individual passenger behaviour is essential for the design MTR transportation, because who can choose to catch bus, taxi, tram, train ferry etc. different kinds of public transportation tools. Individual traveler who decides to catch which kinds of public transportation tools, it depends on whether the public transportation tool can provide real time travel information, liking link travel time schedule. So, MTR underground train needs to understand where it has terminal to give convenience to the local living areas of time travelers to choose to catch MTR easily. Although, MTR ticket fare is one factor to influence any passengers choice. But, those other factors can also influence them to choice. e.g. MTR any terminal location of convenience, short time travelling, none crowding in busy (peak) time, MTR platform waiting arrival time, none sudden MTR engineering machines broken accident events occurrence frequently etc. different factors, any one of these factors which can influence passengers who choose to catch MTR or other kinds of transportation tools.

Why route choice can influence passenger behavioural choice

Usually, the busy time passengers will regard the route choice as a coordination problem to influence them to choose to catch which kinds of transportation tools. The route choice is as an opportunity costs to influence any busy time passengers to decide to choose to catch which kind of transportation tool which is the best right choice in the right time among of them. In the short time, for example, it seems any busy time passengers will choose to catch bus to substitute MTR underground train transportation tool, due to who feels the bus can arrive any destinations to compare other kinds of transportation tools in the most short time. However even if the MTR can either charge cheaper ticket fare to sell full day or charge discount ticket fare to sell in the busy (peak) time to compare to bus fare. It is possible that the busy time passengers will still choose to catch bus, if between the bus terminal and the another bus terminal that distance is the shorter time route to spend time to arrive destination to compare between the MTR terminal to the another MTR terminal arrival time . Also, although the busy time passengers will feel to enounter traffic jam to influence sitting or waiting bus time to be longer time in possible and who also feel MTR can avoid traffic jam problem. However, usually any busy (peak) time passengers will feel the chance of traffic jam occurrence will be less. So, the short bus route choice is more potential factor to influence the busy (peak) time passengers still to choose bus to catch.

However, if anyone wants to investigate results of day-to-day route choice which can be transferred to more realistic environment. It is necessary to explore individual behaviour in an interactive experimental set up to ensure busy (peak) time passenger transportation behavioural choice. For example, a passenger has a choice between a main road (M) and a side road (S) for travelling from (A) to (B). (M) is faster if (M) and (S) are chose by the same number of passengers. So, this method can be researched whether MTR terminal station is located at the main road (M) or the side road (S) where is more suitable to accept to passengers generally.

Why trip time reliability and
crowding factors can influence
MTR passenger choice.

Other problem is MTR busy (peak) time's crowding in public transportation occurrence of MTR underground train transportation tool is becoming a growth to concern as MTR demand growth at a busy (peak) time. To capture the MTR passengers benefits with reduced crowding from improved MTR public transport service and image. It is necessary a identify the relevant dimensions of crowding that are meaningful measures of what crowding means to MTR passengers. Two main influences on MTR model choice that are growing in relevance are trip time reliability and crowding. It represents a benefit-cost framework. In fact, MTR passengers can be willing to pay more expensive ticket fare, it MTR can avoid crowding and short and the accurate arrival trip time between terminals is reliable to occur. How to measure of MTR crowding, e.g. weighting the gap between the busy time, the standard (i.e. objective) and the perceived (i.e. subjective) metrics. We are not in a position to definitely map the two dimensions, which is a crucial requirement for translating objective improvements into equivalent subjective gains that then can be applied, willingness to pay estimates MTR ticket fares to obtain the additional MTR passenger benefits of MTR public transportation investment to any terminal stations. Because MTR crowding has a negative impact on passengers in terms of psychological on emotional distress. MTR passengers are willing to stand for up to 20 minutes of the service is fast and reliable. However crowding outweighed these benefits from a MTR passenger's perpective, experienced crowding leads a increased dissatisfaction. e.g. stress and less privacy during who needs to stand up in MTR. Due to there are no enough places to supply to them to stand up in MTR. If the MTR trip time was longer time between the passenger's terminals, who will feel more dissatisfaction and it will cause who feels whether who ought need to choose to catch other transportation tools to substitute MTR next time. e.g. bus, train, tram, ferry, taxi etc. So, from an operator's perspective, the MTR service frequency or MTR size is significantly influenced by the level of ridership, which sends a signal to respond if the monitored crowding level exceeds the benchmark standard in the busy time. e.g. in the morning time or at the night time, the students or employment people who need to go to schools or offices (working places). The locations of different places between MTR terminals and crowding are regarded as a key service attribute for MTR pubic transportation along with other factors, such as travelling time and reliability, e.g. service quality, none engineering machines are broken to cause MTR stops suddenly.

Given the increasing importance of crowding on both the disutility to existing MTR public transportation users and the influence to it. MTR passenger can choose to use either the MTR public public transportation or other public transportation. It is timely to review the MTR current measures of crowding defined by transportation authorities. MTR operators ought evaluate whether they apporpriately reflect MTR each traveler experiences and perceptions of crowding in busy (peak) time. I suggest that MTR needs to buy other underground trains to supply to the busy (peak) time passengers to let them have enough seats to sit down, so who do not need to stand up in any MTR underground trains when they catch MTR underground trains in busy time. It aims to let who are willingness to pay the estimation of reasonable ticket fares to compare the other kinds of transportation tools in the busy (peak) time.

What is the crowding difference
between train and MTR underground train.
In fact, crowding won't be happened to brother these transportation tools easily in the busy time and non busy time both. e.g. bus, taxi, train, tram,

ferry. Because passengers can not choose to stand up in these transportation tools easily, due to these transportation tools have no enough areas (spaces) to let them to stand up easily . So, the crowding will be avoided to occur in these tranportation tools usually. Otherwise, MTR will have many passengers who can choose to stand up because MTR design of length is very long and it has enough areas (places) to let passengers to choose to stand up, even there have none any seats are provided to let them to sit down. So, MTR passengers will feel more dissatisfaction and crowding easily, especial in any peak (busy) time every day.

Comparing to bus, much more diverse crowding measures are defined in the passenger rail industry. For passenger, different specifications for measuring crowding are found across countries and even within a country. For example, rail crowding measures in the UK, the passengers in excess of capacity is crowding measure that applies to all London and South east operators weekday train services at a London terminus during the morning peak from 0700 to 09: 59 , and those departing during the afternoon peak from 16:00 to 18:59 (office of rail regulation 2011 year). The overall PIXC figure is considered the planned standard class capacity of each train service as well as the actual number of standard class passengers on the service at the critical point. i.e. the location on a trains of standard class passengers that surpass the planned capacity as the difference between the number of actual passengers and the capacity of the train divided by the number of passenger is within the capacity . So, it seems train and MTR underground public transportaton tools had been encountering the crowding problems in peak time, the difference in train passengers need to wait next train or more train arrival is who doesn't plan to enter the train, when who discovers the current train has no seats to provide to them to sit down in whose trip. Otherwise, MTR passengers can choose either to stand up within the large areas (places) if who discovered there are no any seats to provide to them to sit down or who can wait the next MTR arrival in order to who can sit down. It seems MTR transportation tool crowding environment includes in waiting platform and inside of the MTR underground train. Otherwise, train transportation tool crowding environment only includes the waiting platform and the passengers will not have crowding feeling inside of the train, due to none of passengers choose to stand up inside any trains because any train inside has no enough places to let them to stand up.

How MTR can attract many passengers.

On the commuter departure time choice of any reference point researching hand, the departure time decisions of communters are of fundamental importance of peak period MTR traffic congestion. However, whether on the demand side, MTR underground train congestion relief measures, such as MTR ticket fare to every terminal station needs to be charged cheaper fare or discount fare in the peak (busy) time every day. To aim to attract many passengers to choose to catch MTR Underground train public transportation tools, substitute to choose other public transportation tools in the peak time.

Over the past decades, there have been very active research efforts in the departure time problem, both in econometric modeling and dynamic user equilibrium fields. Although, these works provide valuable insights into dynamic commuter decision making, they do not identify the commuters' response to gains and losses related to whole actual arrival time to reference points who may have relative. The appliability of the reference point hypothesis of prospect theory to the commuter's departure time decision making to obtain a better understanding of how departure time choice in MTR platform during their waiting underground train arrival time. However, every MTR underground train actual arrival time and deviation variables related to reference points (gains and losses) are the key factors in the departure time choice model. How the MTR underground train of every communter's daily departure time decision can be modelled when the reference point hypothesis of prospect theory. The MTR underground train's schedule delay is defined as the difference between the preferred arrival time (PAT) and the actual arrival time (AT) for a given MTR communter. In a daily MTR commute, a commuter in the indifference band actual arrival time is an essential feature of MTR schedule study. Two reference points are the earliest acceptable arrival time and the work starting time for a given MTR platform waiting passengers. In psychological view point, prospect theory proposes that the displeasure of a loss is perceived or greater than the pleasure of a gain of the same attitude and therefore, the value function is stronger for losses than gains.

To conclude, it seems that if MTR waiting passengers need not spend long time to wait underground train arrival in platform and it can provide seats to let them to sit down in the busy (peak) crowding time. It will make them to feel pleasure, even the MTR ticket fare is not fair and reasonable to charge higher fare to compare other kinds of public transportation tools fares. So the peak waiting time factor can influence the passengers to choose other kind of transportation tools to catch easily. Moreover, MTR's two reference points are the earliest role. Similarly a loss is observed when the MTR platform waiting commuter experiences or actual arrival time which is beyond that the MTR schedule time. Due to that a MTR waiting commuter is as an early side arrival of whose actual arrival time is earlier than whose preferred arrival time.

Reference

Bailey, L., Mokhtarian, P.L. Little, A. (2008). The broader Connection Between Public Transportation, Energy Conservation And Greenhouse Gas Reduction, Report Prepared As Part Of TCRP Project J-11/Tasks Transit Cooperative Research Program, Transportation Research Board Submitted To American Public Transportation Association in http://www.apta.com/research/into/online/land_use.cfmi, accessed 17 April 2008.

The UK Standing Advisory Committee On Trunk Road Assessment (SACTRA) (1999). Transport And The Economy (Report To UK DETR). Retrieved From: http://webarchive.nationalarchives.gov.uk/20050301192906 ; http://dft.gov.uk/stellent/groups/dft-econappr/documents/pdf/dft_econappr_pdf_022512.pdf

Wikipedia Contributors (2008). Arterial Roads In Wikipedia, The Free Encyclopeda, http://en.wikipedia.org/w/index.php?title=Arterial_road&oldid=212832640(accessed May30,2008).

What the psychological need differences between rail and bus passengers

● Reasons we need to improve public bus transport tool service quality

The ways that we need to improve public transport, e.g. bus transport service, we try our best to ask these questions: During periods of stress on the bus, like weather conditions or maintenance failure that slows the bus service system? How to improve mass transit on bus service frequency, when looking at ways to improve public bus service transport , riders want frequency? Interestingly, speed is not as much of an issue, if they are waiting downtown in the rain, or on some suburban backstreet, riders want to know that a bus will arrive soon, preferably in less than 15 minutes. Therefore, the wait becomes part of the transportation cycle. Even, if the bus is lightning fast, in the mind of the rider, the trip begins right when they arrive at the bus station, and start waiting for the bus to pick them up.

`What does efficient bus ticketing system mean? It is big part of how to improve bus transportation efficiency is improving transit ticketing system, because ticketing systems have to be quick and practical to allow for prompt loading and unloading of passengers. So, inefficient ticketing systems also slow down bus frequency, as drivers need to wait for everyone to tap before they can drive away to the next stop.

How to let passengers feel comfortable? Riders want comfortable buses that can seat as many people as possible. Face-to-face seating is not appealing and being knee-to-knee in a confined space creates awkward moments between strangers. However, comfort also extends beyond the buses' seating arrangements. A smooth riding, quiet bus plays a significant role in reducing the overall stress of a public transit experience. Among the consistent feedback from riders of fuel cell electric buses is a surprised delight about how quiet the buses are when in motion.

On reduce greenhouse gases environment prote3ctoin aspect, exhaust spewing buses are on ongoing concern. One of the significant factors that commuters consider when deciding to take public transit is the environment impact of their alternative transport method. And although a diesel bus packed with 40 people may be less environmentally damaging than 40 separate diesel cars, it will still have negative impacts on both local air quality and the overall climate situation , when given the choice, we've found nearly all riders prefer " zero-emission buses" to conventional diesel buses nowadays.

IN fact, we are always thinking of ways to improve public transportation by dev4eloping new clean fuel technologies. Fuel cell electric buses resolve some of the above issues for both transit bus operators, bus performance is continually being proven and improved over millions of miles of operation in environments ranging from mountain villages to desert communities to busy cities. Hence, the first step to creating better public transit networks is becoming aware of the available options. Many communities are taking measures to improve public transport by implementing innovative sustainable transport solutions that have profound impacts on the live ability of their communities.

So, I shall recommend these ways to improve public transport methods to bus service as below:

Firstly, making interchanging easy for public transport has most efficient public transport service improvement aim at linking areas that are outside a city to the city center., doing this is beneficial in two ways. It helps people who should not at the city center , but needed to pass through because the outlying areas are not connected together to keep off and hence reduce congestion at the center. Also, connecting the outlying areas provide a backup for the public transport system in case of a problem which often happen.

Secondly, minimize the number of stops/ stations, stops and stations improve the efficiency of public transport , but there should be a balance between enabling accessibility with more steps or stations and reducing the costs of operation by increasing transit need of ensure trips are covered in time. Therefore, core should be taken to ensure that stops and stations are located on streets to balance accessibility by commuters on one hand and reduces operating cost on the other hand.

Thirdly, lessen traffic congestion by deploying a number measures. Reducing traffic congestion at city streets could be done, implementing a number of strategies, such as providing lanes dedicated specially for the use of public transport, deploying strict regulations , such as queue bypasses or queue jumps. Another means of reducing traffic congestion is by providing feeds and data from public transport systems, freely to commuters to educate and help them avoid areas of traffic congestion and finally, giving priority to public and trams operating efficiency, increasing the travel time of these engineering mechanism whereby a traffic signal turns green at the light of a public transport at an intersection. All of above these improvements may be future public transport bus passengers service improvement need, if any bus companies hope to increase their bus passengers number absolutely.

- What rail passengers really want rail innovation improvement

Public transport systems, such as rail provides benefits including less traffic congestion, less pollution, safe travels, lower expenditures , less effort and better predictability in comparison to road transport. In fact, bus and train riders experience the most negative emotions in comparison with other transport modes, such as private cars , walking and cycling. Hence, technology has the potential to bring about the changes, needed to increase efficiency of rail transport, e.g. cost-effective ways to improve the quality of public transport and increase ridership may involve comfort and convenience improvement, or technology has the potential to provide more up-to-date information and customized service to train passengers and therefore improve the rail journey experience . On the overall, passenger journey , e.g. the importance of automated traveller information systems, and electronic fare payment collection systems can bring rail passengers look for this information in different interfaces from localized displays installed on platforms to smartphone applications.

Moreover, technology can also improve fare collection and management which of made manually can be prone to error, and time consuming , unified cards, smartphones can make it easier for rail passengers to obtain ticket, with the potential to increase the user satisfaction with the rail system. Because rail passengers demand not only pre-trip information for planning their travels, but also information during journeys, such as punctuality, connections and platform allocation. One extensive review indicates that accurate communication, for example, giving effective way finding information, can optimize passengers' experience with public transport.

Also, technology can facilitate the process of finding free seats on trains, which is a current demand from rail passengers and the cause of stress during the boarding process. IN fact, many rail passengers have specific preferences regarding seats and would appreciate having control of where to sit. So, navigation and way finding information can be delivered directly to passengers to inform where they could stand aiming to board less busy carriages, for example, choosing to travel on a less crowded train, or spreading themselves out on the platform before boarding in respond to crowding information, e.g. smartphones are frequently used by passengers of public transport and can make waiting times seem shorter. Furthermore specific system features designed for train passengers have the potential to improve the journey experience of the travelling public.

What ferry passengers service improvement need

- How can ferry service be improved affordable, reliable, convenient, flexible and clean will get drivers out of their cars ad onto environmentally responsible to passenger ferries?

Ferry transportation provides an environmentally friendly commuting alternative to the congested roadways in many of countries , so ferry transport service needs to meet long term air quality goals, it is critical to move beyond traditional technologies to zero-and near zero emissions technology. Clearly putting a transit system in operation that demonstrates emission control technology and the development of zero-emissions, ferries will help achieve air quality goals to our societies, for example., new shipping rout4es are needed to increase in order to satisfy ferry passengers different rapid ferry journey short distance need, when they need to choose one kind of public transport service either bus or rail or ferry transport service among of them.

None ferry accident occurrence, ferry service needs to let passengers to feel it is the safest sea pubic transit, expanded recreational service is also needs, particularly on weekends when bridge , corridor traffic congestion is becoming an increasing problem. Ferry service needs have uniquely provided flexible, vital transportation supports in response to a natural or man-made disaster that shuts down bridges and roads, fuel –cell technology is needed , that will lead to zero-emissions ferries, e.g. on-board emissions monitoring is far less polluting than previously through, e.g. 149 passenger boats are designed to travel 25 knots or less , and 300-350 passenger vessels designed for speeds up to 30-35 knots.

This emissions standard will perform specifications and the cost of this technology is accounted for in the ferry company vessel capital budget ,e.g. vessel design capabilities to accommodate existing and new docking configurations . This maximizes fast ferry passenger loading, including bicycles, carriages and wheelchairs. Hence, future global ferry service needs have these positive influence to our societies: Need for flexibility, desire to help the environment, need for time saving, which includes the importance of reliability, sensitivity to personal travel experience, such as a need for personal space or quiet feeling ferry seat any time, insensitivity to transport cost, e.g. the ferry ticket price is cheaper than rail or bus fares sensitivity to stress.

However, ferry service is different unlike rail, bus because expanded ferry service can be launched quickly at low initial cost and with great flexibility. Unlike buses, ferries are not hindered by traffic congestion on roads and highways or in tunnels. So, ferry service can be safely expanded to bring new service to new places and add more service to existing routes more easily than bus and rail public transport both, e.g. expanded ferry transport service can operate safety and provide with a robust, flexible and effective emergency response capability if the region is hit with a natural or man-made event that disables roads, other transit, bridges , before any.

Hence, ferry companies need to decide to improve their ferry transport service, they need to answer these questions: Is the new shipping route a good transportation investment? Does the new shipping route have fatal environmental negative impact? Does it offer a transit option that can be initiated in a timely and cost-effective manner? Can it provide ferry transport service that is reliable, safe and fully accessible after the ferry recovery would be unreasonably high charge to ferry selection is decided to implement to increase?

Also, ferry safety is needed to consider because it can influence any ferry passenger choice, when the ferry is moving on the sea, when the passenger is sitting on the boat. The ferry safety issue may include: Ensuring that access to all ferry operational areas, including, machinery spaces, pilothouse and gear lockers, remain locked at all times and accessible only to authorized crew, posting night watch security guards at terminals, conducting diligent onboard inspection for unattended passenger bags, briefcases and packages after each run, before the next boat load is allowed to board, creating coded signals and response to report suspicious activity, requiring positive identification before allowing any contractors, vendors or others access to ferries, providing additional security training to crew, developing a security plan to account for potential threats, outlining preventive measures and detailing an action plan in the event of a threat or actual emergency.

Future Human Transport Need Change

How future our transport need change? What factors influence our future transport need change? In general, these factors may influence our transportation need change. They may include fuel cost, the labor market for commercial drivers, demand for frieight , customer loyalty , vehicle capacity, government regulation, geographical events, the public transport tool reputation to passegners as a merchant. However, the factors that influence the development of transport system in an area? They may include as below:

Environment at the local scale existing hydrographical and geomorphological characteristics are string, factors in transport development, particularly in terms of the technical challenges (bridge, gradients,) they present to construct, other factors may include historical, technological, political and economic factors. All of these factors may influence our future transport system how develops. For raiway development influential factors, they may include: Geograohical factors, e.g. the North Indian plain with its level land, high density of population and rich agriculture presents the most favourable conditions for the development of railways in India. However, the presence of large number of rivers makes it necessary to construct bridges which involve heavy expenditure to Indian Government publich transport expenditure.

How transport has changed from past to present?

There has been a remarkable development in modern transportation. The stream engine and then the stream trains have emerged and spread at this time and in abundance until the discovery of natural gas and oil was an evolution of transportation. Thus, the sedams and vehicles began to run in oil, until present battery changes energy vehicle need, even future non-manual driving artificial intelligent driving vehicle need. These new transport technology may influence our future public transportation from gas energy to battery changed energy, even non-manual driving vehicles need to our daily transport need.

So, our future purpose of public transport need is the unique purpose to oversome space, which is shaped by a variety of human and physical constraints, such as distance, time. These both is our future main public transport need main purpose factors, short distance and reducing journey time, they influence that why we need to choose to catch any kinds of public transportation tool to replace purchase private cars to drive transport tool choice. So, future any kinds of public transport tools, they need to consider above both main factors , how to attract passengers to choose to catch themselves public transport tools choice in this competitive public transport tools market.

On the other hand, the economic importance of transportation development can be defined as improving the welfare of a society, through appropriate social, political and economic conditions , such as US Government spent too much money to assist MTR (MAss transport railway firm) to develop underground thrain transport. Its aim to let many passegner can reduce journey time and reduce distance between destinations, it also hopes US citizen passengers can pay cheap transport fare to buy ticket to catch underground transport train for many families their transport expenditure in social transport welfare view.

However, US Government neds to solve those challenges, before it implements to develop rapid underground railway , e.g. lack of knowledge of geographical fwatures, lack of manpower necessary to operate the rapid underground railway construction work, lack of construction materials within the US itself. For Brazil rail network transportation development example, the factors influence the use of rail network for transportion is highly restricted in Brazil. Thus, the development of roadways and waterways is the main modes of transportation that caould be used in Brazil given its topography and drainage benefit to society . So, brazil can develop rail network for transportation development in success.

So, transportation system is important in the development of any nation, because transportation plays important role in rapid economic growth of a nation. Thrapsortation increases the quality and variety of consumer goods, thereby stimulating the demand and development of trade and economy of the nation. Moreover, transport provides various employment opportunities and boosts up the economy of the country.

Also, any transport tools need to improve themselves transport service in order to attract passengers to choose their public transport service more easily. They may attempt to sign up for an autonomous vehicle pilot program, free phone enquiey concerns whether the passegner can catch which bus bumber to go to the destination, hou much bus fare, how long journey time, when the bus will arrive teh bus stops or leave the bus stop etc. bus service questions, before any one passenger prepares to choose to catch bus (free bus go phone call enquiry), free download a public transport tool transit app. even water taxi tranport tool innovation can replace ferry public transport tool, it can let passengers have more fun an enjoyable catching feeling. So, water taxi tranport tool is one kind of future new transport tool change to replace ferry , it can influence ferry passengers to choose water taxi public transport tool to replace ferry. Although, its fare may be more expsnse to compare ferry, but it can reduce jounrey time and distance between both water stations, when ferry can not arrive the other destinations, but water taxi can arrive any one water station destination. It can bring convenient to future any one ferry passengers. So, water taxi may be developed to some countries, e.g. New Zealand , Auckland city, US , Washington and New York cities they had developed water taxi public transport tools to let ferry passengers have one kind new water public transport choice.

However, instead of new transport innovation improvement to water transport service public transport with input from the public on bus transport service aspect, bus frequency improvement, it means when booking at ways to improve, bus frequency from long times to less times, efficient bus ticketing system, a big part of how to improve tranportation efficiency is improving transit ticketing system.

In fact, my future transport system may still include these five types, modes of transport are: railway, roadways, airways, waterways and piplelines. Also, among different includes of transport, railways are the different modes of transport, railways are the cheapest. Trains cover the distance in less time and comparatively, the fare is also less to other modes of transporation. Therefore, railways is the cheapest mode of transportation to compare ferry, water taxi , sea transport, bus, taxi, road system.

On conclusion, transport price is not the main factor to attract passegners to choose to catch. The importance to have a good public transport system in place. It may be one main factor to help the kind of public transport tool to attract passengers to choose to catch, because a good transport links can widen people's job search area and help them find employment. It can also reduce commuting times and reduce the cost of living, and high skilled workers are more likely to travel across longer distances to work, especially if they are following good job opportunities. So, future any one kind of public transportation tool service provider ought consider how to satisfy working people working time need to shorten journey time to any working places or student learning time need to shorten jounrey times to any schools as well as let they feel comfortable to sit on comfortable chairs or provide free internet service to themselves mobiles , laptops, when they are sitting down or standing up in the kind of public transport . It is the important factor to influence any kind of public transport service in success.

Future Non-Manual driving vehicle How
Influences Public Transport Tool Passenger Need

Nowadays, artifical intelligent (non-manual) driving vehicles are invented, it may be accepted to any countries families to feel comfortable to drive on roads, because any people choose to buy any kinds cars, when any people choose to buy kinds of non-manual (artificial intelligent) vehicles, they do not need to use their hands to drive cars, because artificial intelligent (robotic auto control wheels, it means that robots can help human (drivers) to control wheel to drive to avoid any cars crash occurrence on the roads more easily.

If one day, non-manual driving robotic control whoole vehicles are invented in successful, whether it will persuade many different conuntries families choose to buy non-manual (robotic auto control wheel) vehicles, then it will cause bus, tram, train, underground train, road transport need will be influenced to reduce or even if non-manula boats are invented, whether it will cause ferry sea transport needs will b influenced to reduce. Hence, future non-manual driving vehicles or bats invention whether they will influence public transport tool of road and sea transport passengers number reduces. It is one interesting question. I shall attempt to discuss as below:

In fact, non-manual vehicles are very attraction, to excite any person chooses to buy to drive, because people do not need often touch wheels and touch foots button to control cars to move often forever, when robotic can be invented to help human to control car wheel and foot button, any person only needs to sit on his/her car, then the car can move rapidly, because any drivers is lazy, he/she hopes machine can help her/him to drive car on the road safely. So, he/she can read book or listen music or eatch mobile movie to enjoy his/her entertainment when he/she is sitting on his/her car.He/ she will feel more comfortable and enjoyable when robotic can help him/ her to drive car. So, robotic (non -manual driving vehicle) can encourage people to choose to buy cars because any drivers won't need to drive cars, robotic can help drivers them to drive on the road easily, when global any one family can own one robotic auto control (non-manual driving) car at least, it may influence these owning non-manula diriving vehicle owners do not feel need to pay any fares to buy road public transport tools of bus ticket, train ticket, underground train ticket , tram ticket to go to anywhere. So, it seems that robotic (non-manual driving) vehicles may influence future any road transport passengers number reduces , because traditional catching any kinds of road public transport tool passengers will be influenced to choose to sit themselves auto (non-manual) driving cars to go to offices to work, parents do not need to follow their sone/daughters to sit on themselves non-manual auto driving cars to go to schools, because their sons/daughters can sit on themselves non-manual driving cars to go to schools more easily. In holidays, they can sit on themselves non-manual driving cars to go to cinemas, music halls, breachs, theaters, shopping centers, gardens different entertainment places to enjoy their any leisure safely because robotic can help them to drive their cars on roads safely.

So, it means that robotic auto control driving cars can influence global every family to feel that they do not need to catch any kinds of public transport tools, e.g. bus, train, tram, taxi underground train to go to anywhere because robotic auto driving cars can help any one, he/she does not know how to drive car to go to anywhere safely. So, future any one won't need to learn driving car skill, when he/she likes to buy one auto driving car. So, in passenger public transport need view, non-manual driving cars will influence them to feel any kinds of road public transport tools can help them to go to anywhere conveniently, because themselves non-manual driving vehicles can help them to drive cars to go to anywhere conveniently. They only need to tell robotic that where they want to go, when they sit on their non-manual driving cars, then robotic knows whether where destination, they want to go, their cars will auto move on the road immediately. It is one exciting and enjoyable ourney when the driver does not need to drive his/her car on the road. So, it seems that robotic (non-manual driving) vehicles invention may bring negative influence to any kinds of public transport tools service needs to passengers , when passengers had owned one non-manual driving car at least.

Why and how non-manual driving car owners need

raise public transport quality on travel time and fare

aspects

● How non human driving behavior can be influence by non-manual driving cars

In fact, impact of automated vehicless on travel mode preference, it can bring both trip purposes and distances aim raising need to any kinds of public transport service passegners. Because of technology penetration in the transportation system, the automated vehicle is set to be a future mode of transport, it may bring negative impact to future any kinds of public transport passengers needs, in special on the potential impact of these non-manual driving automated vehicles on travel behaior negative impact to public transport passenger behavior. Automated vehicles will influence future public transportation passengers feel it can bring more short time travel distances and short trip purposes more benefit than any kinds of public transport choices, e.g. bus, taxi, ferry, train, tram, underground tram etc. road and sea public transport tools, e.g. ferry, water taxi. It means that when future any passenger feels above these any one kind of public transport tool needs to spend longer travel time on journey distance and trip to compare future automated vehicles, then they will choose to sit on automated vehicles in preference, due to automated vehicles can help global any one person needs to go to anywhere rapidly.

So, automated vehicles may replace general traditional public transport tools in possible, when they are popular accepted in societies. On the other, instead of shortening journey travel distance time, (travel time) aspect, public transport fare, travel cost will be another influential factor to influence future public transport tool passengers to choose automated vehicles to replace to catch any kinds of public transport tools.

In fact, conventional cars and public transport s are perceivd as being the least attractive alternative in relation to in-vehicle travel time on short and long distance communting trips. So , future automated vehicle drivers (non -human driving) behaviors will be likely changed to prefer this mode for long distance leisure trips rather than short distance commuting trips by automated vehicles.

In fact, advanced technologies have revolutionized many aspects of human life, include the automated vehicle transport system. Also, transport system is one of the essential development aspect to particular , such as non-manual driving automation , vehicle aims to make trips safer, faster , more efficient, automated vehicles passengers and drivers can feel enjoyable to do themselves leisure behavior , e.g. read books, listen, music, listen mobile, watch laptop movies when any one does not need to consider whether their cars are safe to be driven , even any one needs to drive the automated car, because robotic can help them to control how to automatic drive this car on the road safely.

Robotic will bring confidence to let them feel that themselves cars are moving safely on the roads . In recent years, the concept of automated driving has been introduced as on outstanding platform for the next generation of driving systems that is expected to improve safety, traffic flows efficiency, reducing traffic jams occurrence chance, avoiding traffic accidents occurrence chance, e.g. avoid to crash any one person when he/ she is walking across road or crach any car is moving on the road easily, capacity, accessibility , and reducing congestion through the application of some technologies , such as vehicle to vehicle and vehicle to infrastructure communication.

So, future automated vechicles can have good driving facility systems to be installed in their cars, in order to raise safety, rapid driving speed level to let any one to feel , when they are sitting in their automated cars, e.g. using cameras, sensors, global positioning system adaptive cruise control, light detection and ranging, and advanced driver assistance system, automated vehicles can steer the vehicle and drive it automatically when passengers delegate control to a computer. Absolutely, ny replacing the driver role with an automated driving system , future one automated vehicle is able to totally free up passengers under automation levels.

So, unless future any kinds of public transport tools may apply automated robotic automated driven system replace the bus driver, taxi driver, train driver, tram driver, underground train driver to raise automated driving system service improvement level to let any one passengers to feel. Otherwise, when automated vehicles are popular to be accepted to buy in any one country in global. Then, global public tansport tool passegners number may be influenced to reduce when global any one family owns at least one automated vehicle at themselves homes .

In other words, automated vehicles can bring thes benefits to let global any one household family feels, future automated vehicles users , they can mostly behave like passengers inside the vehicle, which implies that they will be able to multitask and productive by allocating the travel time to do other activities, e.g. reading, eating, working, drinking, watching movies, listening musics, even sleeping. So, automated vechicles will motivate humans to change non-humanly driven behaviors from conventional humanly driven behavior. This non-humanly driven behavior may be one main factor to influence or encourage future any one kind of public transport passenger won't choose to pay fare to buy ticket to catch any one kind of public transport tool again, because non-manual driven behavior may hel many lazy people do not need to consdierate how to learn to drive cars skills to prepare pass any road test in order to earn the driving licnece to permit to drive cars forever. When automated vehiclesa re popular to be accepted to replace manual-driven cars in societies.

Hence, automated vehicles could potentially change the traditional human driven vehicle market to cause their manual driven cars sale buyers number reduces, when the automated vehicle buyers number increases, also they can chance globa public transport passengers behaviors to reduce to pay fares to catch any kinds of public transport tools when automated vechicles users may sit on themselves automated vehicles to go to anywhere in short time rapidly and safely in any countries.

On conclusion, future global public transport service competition is serious, because instead of global passengers had began to compare whether which kinds of public transport fares are cheaper, more safe, shortening journey time between leaving place and destination, more comfortable feeling, e.g. clean and comfortable chairs , mre free internet service facilities in order to make any one kind of catching public transport tool choice in preference. On the other hand, future automated vehicles number will increase when traditional manual driven car users begin to believe that automated vehicles can bring more safe , more comfortable, more fee-time using, more leisure satisfactory feeling, more than traditional manual driving cars. Then, when global any one household family had made choice to buy at least one automated vehice to replace themselves car(s) at home. When, they are habit to sit in themselves automated vehicles to go to anywhere, however, short or long trip . Consequently, global any one household family won't feel any kinds of public transport tools may bring personal economic saving cost, comfortable, enjoyable, free-time using benefit to compare themselves automated vehicles . It will cause global public transport tools passengers number will reduce , when many different kinds of home automatic vehicles are purchased to replace manual driving cars by global household automated vehicle users. So, in passegner transport tool choice psychological view, automatic vehicles will be possible to replace future public transport service tools. So, any public transport service providers can not neglect how to desing and improve their facilities , charge reasonable transport fare, provide more comfortable, and enjoyable sitting feeling , even applying automatic driving system to replace human drivers in order to attract passegners ' catching need choice more easily.

Artificial Intelligent In Road Transportation Strategy

- How artificial intelligent vehicle may interact intelligent transportation tools

Can artificial intelligence (AI) and machine learning (ML) be used in the search for new " consumption" behavioral type variables that affect consumer individual or transportation service organization individual different transportation tools choices, such as road or sea or sky transportation tools? Can artificial intelligent vehicle may interact intelligent transportation tools market development?

Consumers usually have bargaining and on risk choice when they are already shopping, such as who need to accept to use any (AI) new technological products to replace human traditional behaviors, such as intelligent non-manual driving transportation market, e.g. cars are needed to be driven by human drivers on road, but it has bargaining and on risky choice, when non-manual (AI) vehicle buyers who need to depend on non-manual artificial intelligent (ML) system assists them to drive their cars on the roads.

So, any non-manual driving auto car buyers must need to believe (AI) non-manual driving vehicles (ML) systems can make accurate driving judgement to reduce or avoid any traffic accident occurrences more than human drivers' driving judgement when the (ML) systems are driving their cars on the roads. Then the intelligent vehicle manufacturers will have possible to sell their non-manual driving vehicles success.

This is the first reason or idea influences consumer individual choice to buy any kinds of (AI) non-manual driving vehicles, when consumers believe (ML) systems are more safe and make more accurate judgement to compare human or computer systems, when they are sitting in one non-manual auto driving vehicle on the road.

The another second reason or idea is that some common limits on driving consumer prediction might be understood as the kinds of errors made by poor implementation of machine learning.

Supposing driving consumers believe (AI) machine learning ability is worse to compare to human learning ability. It will also influence driving consumers do not accept to use any (AI) non-manual auto driving vehicles to replace every driver is essential on driving by himself/herself on the road. The third idea or reason is that it is important to influence driving customers believe how (AI) non-manual auto driving technology is used in them can both overcome and exploit human driving skill and safe limits and raise more auto driving safe judgement to compare human driving safe judgement.

However, how to predict any kinds of (AI) non-manual driving vehicles future consumption effort, due to different kinds of (AI) non-manual driving transportation vehicles which have different unique functions and designs to be used by different kinds of road transportation or driving demand of consumers. For example, lorry drivers need non-manual intelligent system can help them to drive fast, but safe to assist them to transport cargo to arrive destinations from their factories or offices. Otherwise, private car driver expects whose (AI) non-manual driving vehicle can auto drive to send to whom to arrive destination in safe way and non-too fast and non-too slow speed in order to avoid accident occurrences.

So, a different road intelligent consumer demand is to define whose individual driving behavior and driving habit and driving attitude and driving judgement and driving speed demand to decide how to design whose intelligent vehicle to satisfy those driving demand more generally, as simply being open-minded about what variables are likely to influence every consumer economic choice, when who decide either to buy any kinds of (AI) products or not to buy any kinds of (AI) products to replace the different demand of consumers their different (AI) useful demand.

Hence, for these three (AI) products group of stakeholders, such as home (AI) consumer group, firm (AI) consumer group and government (AI) consumer group . These consumer groups may consider whether different kinds of (AI) products can give what is special beneficial interest to them to use. These variables can be measurable properties of choices to influence them to choose to buy any (AI) kinds of (AI) products to use, e.g. psychophysiological, biological, social influences, consumer's wealth, moods and personality, (AI) product price etc. variable factors which will influence them to decide to attempt to buy any kinds of (AI) products to use.

If behavioral economics is as open-mindedness about what variables might predict. Then , (AI) machine learning system is a way to do behavioral economics because it can make use of a wide set of variables and select-which ones predict.

In behavioral economic view point, when general consumer overall demand to the product is much than the other similar (AI) non auto driving vehicle products, such as any kinds of (AI) non-manual auto driving vehicles and any kinds of manual driving vehicles case, then any kinds of (AI) non-manual auto driving vehicles will be more attractive to cause many manual driving vehicle buyers choose to buy (AI) non-manual auto driving vehicles. Hence, it seems if any kinds of (AI) non-manual auto driving vehicle products can make more attractive variable efforts to influence overall driving consumers to feel that they have more needs to drive non-manual auto vehicles to compare more than driving manual driving vehicle.

What is the main variable effort to intelligent vehicles to attract driving consumers to choose to accept to drive them ? However, I believe that (AI) machine learning system is a main factor to raise overall driving consumers' acceptances to drive it to replace manual driving vehicle. If it can persuade or prove (AI) machine learning system ability and judgement effort is more accurate than human or computer learning effort or judgement effort, then it is possible that any kinds of (AI) non-manual driving vehicle products will be accepted to drive on the road in popular.

Machine learning system is able to find prediction value in details of how the bargaining occurs. This discovery is the beginning of the next step for driving consumer individual driving behaviors or driving habits. It raises questions that include: What variables predict to influence driving consumers to change whose driving habits or driving attitudes? How can driving consumer individual emotion, face-to-face talking with whose friends when they are sitting in the non-manual driving vehicle to influence whom driving habit or driving attitude to be changed ? Do driving consumers consciously understand why those habit driving attitudes variables are important when they are sitting in one intelligent vehicle? Can (AI) driving machine learning methods capture the effects of motivated cognition to influence driving consumers decide to buy any kinds of (AI) non-manual auto vehicle products more attractively. So, it seems (AI) driving machine learning method is a main variable factor to influence driving consumers to feel who have more confidence to drive them more than any other kinds of similar manual driving vehicles on the road.

Consequently, (AI) driving machine learning system will be one important psychological method to influence driving consumers to choose to buy (AI) auto driving vehicle products to replace manual driving vehicles. The reason is because human and driving machine learning system both which will have limited variable factors to influence general different countries (AI) driving consumers' need desire to be raised.

● Why can (AI) driving machine learning system main factor influence driving consumer individual desires ?

Driving consumer expectations are hard to measure or predict driving attitudes and driving behaviors in (AI) non-manual driving vehicles market. Artificial intelligence is another kind of computer science development to apply intelligent vehicle market. Why do driving consumers feel need to buy any kinds of (AI) auto driving vehicles to drive to replace manual driving vehicles on the roads? What are (AI) auto driving features different to manual driving features?

(AI) is the recreation of cognitive functions in computers; it enables machines to perform tasks like humans and perhaps even better than human. In the real world, scientists develop the technological singularity, in which a superintelligence emerges with unfold human consequences.

Professionals in many industries are intensely interested in the specifics of what (AI) can do today, and how can it helps. They are considering the impact of applied (AI), in which computers are used to address a particular problem, extracting and utilizing patterns found in large volumes of data. Of all (AI)'s subfields, machine learning is attracting the most attention. I shall explain why (AI) machine learning system is the main factor to lead consumers feel need to buy any (AI) products to use. Such as below:

For smartphone, fraud detection to medical diagnosis etc. applied (AI) technological products examples. (AI) machine learning systems can help any one of these products to do any exceed general computer learning systems which (AI) learning systems can do any skills to supply (AI) users to use to compare computer learning systems can not do any skills to supply compute users to use. It seems that (AI) machine learning system is the unique feature to attract consumer consideration in technological product market.

An term for different types of learning, and can be accomplished using different techniques. This has led to a perception that all marketing teams should have (AI) to bring a unified personalized customer experience, when consumers choose to buy any (AI) products to feel what are the different or unique characteristics to compare general computer products. Such as (AI) product has this unique machine learning characteristics, we can predict (AI) and machine learning is connected to influence consumers to feel needs.

Furthermore, over the same time period, and in contrast to predictions for roles in many industries. (AI) won't take the place of marketers and merchandisers themselves although it is already a new value to analytical and strategic marketing skills to persuade consumers to buy any (AI) products. It means different kinds of (AI) products will have different machine learning effort and unique characteristics to attract consumers to choose to buy them to use. Such as, when intelligent vehicles need have unique road driving or sea transportation or flying machine learning system when they are applied on these three kinds of transportation tool aspects. They need have good response safety driving and immediate response learning systems to avoid any boats or air planes or vehicles to crash to them to reduce accident occurrences immediately on any one of either road or sky or sea journey environment.

What is the reason why (AI) driving machine learning system can influence good at making sense to driving consumer desire? Only humans (drivers) , preferably experienced, well informed humans can understand their driving customer needs and decide how to design or reengineer any

(AI) intelligent vehicle product functions. (AI) intelligent vehicle can give these professionals the means to do this better to compare manual driving immediate response control function when any vehicles are driving or they will stop immediately to close / near to them in order to reduce crash occurrence on the road, and then maximize relevance through real-time customization of the non-manual auto vehicle driving user experience.

For example, as ever, senior decision makers need to be informed, decisive and results-oriented or risk losing out. Harvard Business Review indicated : Over the next decade, (AI) won't replace managers, but managers who use (AI) will replace those who don't. Such as intelligent vehicle won't replace drivers, but drivers who use intelligent vehicles will replace those who can not control how to drive their vehicles in the most safe way. So, (AI) driving machine learning system will have possible to do any drivers' (human's) driving judgement, driving analytical mind and driving effort to be more accurate than manual driving skills. Such as how to control to drive the intelligent vehicle in the most safe way. It is general manual driving skill can not achieve to drive in the safe way.

For another (AI) digital commerce example, (AI) and machine learning are the most exciting developments in marketing and merchandising to be applied to digital commerce, such as making better decisions through trend and cluster analysis, deploying product and content in mutually reinforcing combinations, increasing customer engagement and satisfaction in real time.

Hence, the key attraction in digital commerce circles is that machine learning is designed to be self-optimizing. Optimizing for revenue example will surface are increasingly profitably selection of products (within the brand parameters selected).

When to apply (AI) capabilities and what value (AI) is delivering for customer and company like. Unlike any technology before it, (AI) is analytical and predictive capabilities offers the prospect for each and every individual. It can maximize real time and engagement. Effective tailored (AI) technology, such as digital experience cloud technology is available now. And once integrated, (AI) starts learning and delivering incremental value from day one. So (AI) could transform the digital experience to any business organizations.

Hence, (AI) driving machine learning system can be applied to road driving skill aspect. When intelligent vehicles are invented to own the most safe driving judgement skill and they can know when either they may auto drive fast speed, when they are feeling to know when there are not many vehicles are moving close/near to them or when they need auto drive slow speed, when they are feeling to know when there are many vehicles are moving close/ near to them. Then driving consumers will have more confidence to choose to buy any kinds of intelligent vehicles to replace manual driving vehicles to drive on the roads.

● Non-manual driving transportation tool market development

If Non-manual driving vehicle manufacturers expect their (AI) automatic vehicles can attract drivers to buy. I feel them to need to consider how (AI) driving machine learning system can achieve these requirements in order to satisfy manual driving vehicle drivers' requirement to change their traditional driving habit to choose non-manual driving needs. It means (AI) driving machine learning systems can help them to drive vehicles to replace manual driving vehicles on the road. This is the main factor to influence car buyers choose to buy intelligence driving vehicles replace to manual driving vehicles. I believe (AI) non-manual driving vehicle machine learning systems, need to be designed as below:

(1) Improving driving safety by preventing accidents from happening.
Every year, drivers are facing a large number of casualties, due to traffic accidents. The amount of killed and injured road traffic related accidents is increasing every year. The real cost of an accident can go well beyond the limits of immediate material destruction, and is impossible to evaluate.
Hence, researchers and car manufacturers are looking for solutions in order to reduce the amount of accidents. They already developed a considerable set of technologies in order to decrease the amount of casualties. Most of them (like airbags, seat-belts, anti-lock systems, shock absorbing car bodies) are efficient in decreasing the impact of an accident, and in protecting the passengers of the cars. The technologies already saved a lot of lives, but they are rarely able to avoid accidents because they do not anticipate them. Moreover, if they are protecting in many cases, the passengers of the car, they do not prevent most traffic participants, like pedestrians on bicyclists from getting injured. it causes (AI) non-manual automatic car manufacturers need to consider how to design machine learning safety system is to prevent accident from happening instead of just reducing their impact.
This can only be possible using intelligent systems that can observe the

driving environment, reason and decide if there is a danger, determine how to avoid it and act if necessary

(2) Reducing energy consumption by optimizing the driving.

Nowadays, global air pollution is serious. (AI) non-manual driving car manufacturers need to concern how to design (AI) machine learning system can reduce degree of air pollution to be the most minimum level to compare to traditional manual driving vehicles.

The reduction of energy consumption if certainly one of the main challenges. Transportation is one of the major factors in fossil energy consumption, and it is also responsible for a large amount of CO2 pollution. It is difficult to ask individuals to voluntarily limit the use of their vehicle of they do not have a strong incentive to do so. Specially in regions where vehicles are needed to drive to go to work every day. It stands to reason that if it is difficult to decrease the amount of vehicles, part of the solution is to make them more energy efficient.

Hence, non-manual driving car manufacturers need to design how to improve engines, which are more optimized and need less fuel to operate, and hybrid and electric cars have been developed and are continuously being improved. But we can go beyond these solutions that do not take into account the environment in which a vehicle is driving. A growing number of scientific contributions presented intelligent systems used in order to improve energy efficiency and reduce fuel consumption, based on the optimization of the way (AI) non-manual driving (AI) vehicles are performing. Such as recharge batteries and electric engine will be predicted the popular fuel in order to limit fuel consumption to future (AI) non-manual driving vehicles. They can reduce air pollution, consume less fuel for (AI) non-manual driving vehicles.

(3) Improving comfort by anticipating (AI) non- manual driving vehicle drivers.

Finally, another application for intelligent vehicle is the improvement of driving comfort. Car industry is very competitive market. Many potentials (AI) intelligent vehicle customers need to enjoy to sit more comfortable intelligent vehicles, who will be attracted by (AI) comfortable systems improving when driving, so part of the research in intelligent systems from cars focuses on how to improve the driving experience, i.e. make it easier and more enjoyable, more comfortable to compare to traditional manual driving vehicles.

As an example, lane keeping assistant systems are technologies that actively

keep the vehicle in the lane in highways of the driven drifts out of it. Automatic speed regulation keeps the car at a certain speed without requiring to touch the gas pedal. This can be really interesting for, e.g. (AI) non-manual driving truck drivers that spend a lot of time on highways. But these technologies have a limitation in the case of automatic speed regulation, this technology can not copy of a vehicle ahead drives slower than the desired speed, or if another vehicle cuts into the lane.
This case requires the driver to have a constant focus on the road. In order to achieve more comfort, it is better of the system can adapt to changes in its dynamic environment: let the (AI) intelligent vehicle adapt to the speed of the man-manual vehicle, or autonomously change lane when requires. Again, this requires knowledge about the environment, detection capabilities, reasoning and action planning. Intelligent systems can be used in order to create more attractive and more comfortable and more safe, less energy consumption and less fuel expenditure by intelligent vehicles.

HOW DESIGNING UNDERGROUND MASS TRANSIT RAILWAY TO BRING PASSENGERS

- Designing transportation system advantages

Nowadays, transportation and economic development have close relationship. Economic development stimulates transportation demand by increasing the numbers of workers commuting to and from work, customers traveling to and from services areas, and products being moving by lorries on the roads between products and customers. According to Bailey, Mokhtarian and Little (2008) indicated ''transportation route is past of distinct development pattern or road network and mostly described by regular street patterns as an important factor of human existence, development and civilization. The route network combined with increased road transportation investment result in changed levels of conveniently reflected through cost benefit analysis, savings in travel time, and other benefits. " These benefits are noticeable in increased catchment areas for services and facilities , shops, schools, offices, banks and leisure activities.
What are the crisis of neglection to care transporation system ? Why do any countries need to design road transportation system? For example, the Japan country lacks design road trsnaportation system effectively. So, the crisis of road traffic fatalities will raise and the econominc influence will be changed. The crisis indicates more than 7,000 people die annually as a result of motor vehicle crashes in Japan. Driving when under the influence

of alcohol is the leading cause of motor vehicle crash fatalities in both developed and developing countries. So, alcohol is the most serious factor to raise personal risk when drivers are driving in Japan. However, a number of studies have shown that deterring drink driving is an important way to cause fatalities. There is a demonstrative need for social change in Japan.

Japan has recently strengthened its already strict laws in order to reduce the number of alcohol related road fatalities. Those deforms lowered the legal blood alochol contant limit increased, the penalties for offenders. The Japan road traffic legal needs. Any driving a motor with a alcohol limit of 0.03 or higher Japan's maximum sentence is up to 3 years imprisonment or a fine not exceeding 500,000 yen dollars. Is law impact to reduce drinking alcohol to drive in Japan? What are economic influence of the crisis of road traffic fatalities in Japan?

The rational choice theory of offending suggests that offenders are active decision makers who influence a large number of variables into decision whether or not to commit an offence. On the cost-benefit analysis, it is the punishment a possible jail, large fines worth is the reward the convenience of driving home without the expause of a taxi and innovenience to the alcohol drivers in Japan. Instead of law reforms when it detects alcohol in the air exhaled from the alcohol and other offenders and it educates children about the dangers of drinking and it also explains why alcohol driving can also threaten drivers' life when who are drinking alcohol and driving behaviour in the same time in Japan.

On the economic influence hand, implementation of the policy deregulating alcohol sales and alcohol production did not appear to increase traffic fatalities among adult or teenage males or females in Japan. We found that male adult fatalities demonstrated a statistically significant decline following enactment of the deregulation policy in 1994 year. So, Japan implement law to threaten alcohol drinking behaviour is useful. It can influence the alcohol availability and consumption, alcohol production and sales, the 24 hours operated convenience stores or liquor discount stores incomes to be reduced. Even, Japan overall GDP is also reduced from the deduction of liquor alcohol production and sale, also the occurrence of traffic accident fatalities chances will be also reduced.

The Japanese economy has entered a rapid process of liberalization since the mid-1990 year. Many sectors previously under direct government control are now regulated by the competitive market place. The Japanese alcohol beverage market has changed. The entry of cheaper import alcohol products resulted in a encouragement of alcohol consumption to Japan drinking drivers and an raising of increasing of more import alcohol products supply to Japan. Although, it is beneficial to Japan GDP growth. But it also raise the occurrence of chance to traffic accidents rate to cause alcohol drinkers to be death or hurt when who choose drinking alcohol to drive at the same time in Japan. So, alcohol import can bring more consumption, but it can also raise many traffic accidents occurrence in Japan in the same time.

In conclusion, alcohol is not good for health to drink when the consumer often buys alcohol at drink habitually. So, if many Japanese, including the alcohol driving consumers and the alcohol non drinking consumers both who often buy different countries alcohol to drink daily. It will cause their bodies to be unhealth for long term in Japan. It is possible to increase Japan's government's medical expenses to assist the low income or poor people in the future. So, although alcohol import can raise Japan GDP growth in the short term, but it also raise Japan government's medical expenditure to the low income or poor Japanese long term in the future, So it's economic benefit will not good in the future if Japan still import much alcohol to sell in its country.

Many commercial users depend on road transport facilities, with movement of products and services from place to place on the roads, aspect of global and urban economic survival. Hence, developments of various transportation modes have become important to physical and economic developments. For example, urban locations with such relative advantages are found where different transport routes with high degree of connectivity, within the intra and inter urban road networks. On similarly, commercial activities like banking, retail/wholesale businesses and professional services can take advantage of nearness to concentration of activities attracted consumers service providers. This partly caused increase in demand for commercial space and its effects on commercial property values along commercial roads can be rose. However, some countries' roads need to provide pedestrian movements more than the businesses activities, e.g. shorten the time of lorries parking on the road to let pedestrian movements on the narrow road. If the country government did not consider the roads need to let more pedestrian movements or shorten the time of lorries parking on the road. It will cause traffic jam or traffic density of the individual roads. Hence, governments need to concern the locations of commercial property buildings and the relationship between the explanatory variables of the design road networks.

What are construction of roads design networks benefits? In fact, construction of roads increased substantially with the opening up of residential environments that also is getting much benefits from increasing demand for spaces in commercial properties. Many private companies, retail stores, commercial banks aggregate in the main roads of cities, which get advantage of opportunities afforded by locations near central of cities to attract many pedestrians concerning their businesses existence. This led to high concentration of vehicular and pedestrian movements. Specially along the access main roads in the central of cities. The main roads exhibits linkages to form networks of minor routes along which commercial properties locate. If commercial users are displaced residential users, causing sites to be at the highest and best uses with increases in the values of commercial properties. However, it seems road network development is affected by the compact nature of various routes that sometimes causes volume of traffic jam. Thus, demand for transport can't be treated solely as a derived demand road. Improved main and minor roads access an city or rural areas is a necessary (but not sufficient). Precondition for increased productivity, the UK Standing Advisory committee On Trunk Road Assessment (SACTRA, 1999) noted "various ways in which transport can affect economic growth, for example benefits include through reorganization and rationalization of production, distribution and land use: reducing labor costs by expanding catchment areas etc."

What is land use and road transport design system relationship? Land use refers to the whole range of human activity and of the built environment, and to some aspects of the natural environment. This is a way relationship between land use and road transport. Governments need to design how to use land and how to design road transportation systems. e.g. where are built the main roads and/or where are built the minor roads are the most suitable locations in the cities or rural areas ? If the main roads is located in the not suitable locations at the centers of the cities or rural, it will case the increasing traffic volumes and levels of congestion, including air pollution, noise, ground water pollution from run-off , loss of soil functions and loss of bio-diversity to natural environment. By influencing the spatial structure of locations in the urban environment, so land use planning can help to mitigate any negative effects resulting from land use changes.

Modelling and land use transportation interactions has become an important aspect of road design transport planning. On the one side, for example, design roads in urban centers, it can increase land use and it can also reduce employees or students catching buses or driving cars' time spending to go to workplaces or schools users. Hence, the land use and roads designing transportation can give benefits to residents and employment people to reduce time to wait buses or taxies etc. public transportations to go to workplaces or schools or shopping centers etc. anywhere. It seems to assist bus companies or taxi drivers to earn more income, On the other side, designing urban transport systems is also important . Increased densities mean more destinations become within convenient walking and cycling distances and consequently the use of these modes tends to be higher. Also in dese cities public transport systems are able to offer higher levels of service and operate more economically, when the provision of sufficient road space to meet potential demand becomes impractical. It aims to reduce the danger of driving or walking in urban areas. The transport modes (that is walking, cycling, public transport) and the extent of car dependence is less, due to driving users dependency is less on rural roads. Hence, building main roads can concentrate on designing convenience to pedestrian walking to close to their houses on the streets. However, poor transport design and land use can cause to spend too expenditure not only transport costs on governments and transport users both and also the costs of providing other services. These include the usual utilities and also education and health services as well as negative externalities , such as greenhouse gas emissions. Most such studies concluded that there are significant financial and economics cost advantage of inner city redevelopment compared with fringe development.

However, such policies won't necessarily be successfully, in particular because of the two ways road problem, they may result in additional private investments and employment opportunities flowing into the region, buy may equally result in population and employment opportunities flowing out of the target region because of the improved access to other centers. Hence governments need to analyze how to arrange the land use to assist the property developers to choose where are the suitable locations to build offices or factories or shopping centers or houses at capital or urban cities to adapt to whose the growth of living population. For example, to judge where the land use whether where main roads or junior roads are built where are the suitable locations to satisfy the lorry drivers to park their lorries are the safe locations ; to design the minor roads to let the pedestrians to feel no danger to walk on the streets when the cars are driven to near to the streets on the minor roads. Thus, the factor of choosing where the land use to design the main or minor roads areas, sizes and lengths and of the minor or major roads can influence the drivers and pedestrians feel safe or dangerous when who are driving whose cars on the roads or who are walking on the streets to arrive the offices, schools, cinemas, church, houses etc. destination.

● How to let passengers feel impact of undergrouund train transport to their
working time efficiency

Any countries must need road, sea and air transport to assist businessmen to transport products in local or overseas. If the country's road , sea or air transport system service quality is poor. It will influence any products transport time, speed, inefficient transport to anywhere.
How to raise the country's transport system in order to improve efficiencies to let any businessmen can deliver their products to anywhere easily,e.g. warehouses, client homes, supermarkets destination in the most short time to avoid delay occurrence to let clients feel unsatisfactory or complaint their perform their delivery services poorly. I shall discuss the factors how to improve any countrues' transport systems to achieve the most efficient way as below:

Any countries' transport systems will create economic value, e.g. demonstrate value for money, economic worth, viable commercial worth, financial affordable worth, achieveable worth. Any countries' transport systems can bring welfare value by economics. It has direct relationship to take the form of measured economic activity, i.e. GDP. The form of measured economic activity can impact on any countries' economic economic geography, locally , regionally and nationally's local GDP impacts. The welfare impacts may include: leisure time savings, e.g. the local people drive cars or catch any public transportation tools to go to any geogrpahical location's shopping centers, big gardens, swimming pools, cinemas etc. places to carry on any kinds of leisure activities.

Environmental impacts may include avoiding noise, air pollution on road transportation aspect , when the main road is only on on focus on the main city,
but the city lacks other roads to let any drivers can choose them to drive, instead of the main road in the city. Then, when many cars are driven on the busy transport
time, e.g. morning working time or night busy time between 6:00 and 9:00

AM, between 6:00 and 9:00 PM. When either many working people need to catch public transport or drive themselves cars to go to offices to work or they need to catch pubic transport tools or drive themselves cars to home. Then, the only one main road problem will need them to stay themselves cars on roads, due to traffic jam or traffic accidence occurrence problem causes when many cars are driven on the road in the busy transport time. It will influence they can not go to offices or homes easily daily, even in the busy transport time, their cars' gas need to be used much to cause air pollution and traffic noise is easily caused easily in the busy transport time on the road. When the city has only one main road for drivers in the busy transport time. So, poor road transport system can bring poor impact on economic welfare benefits arising from proved labour supply from commuting, time savings, including exchequer benefits. Consequently, the county's GDP will be fallen down, due to labour market effects which do not add to welfare value.

Whether can poor transport system impact indirectly on GDP or not on local, regional , or national economic geography impacts? Does transport lead to greater economic activity i.e. higher GDP? DO they lead to change in economic activity location? Does transport impact the existence of business location and new economic activity opportunities? The measurement on every country's transport how impacts on economic change, facilitating geographic division of labour and specialization. It can be analyzed on these general aspects:

Costs and speed of travel time (Economic value of travel time savings) . Travel time savings to users from improved transport is a key of economic value, but it has only less influence,journey time reliability is more important to business frieght as well as business travellers, network connectivity enhancements as well as business travellers, network connectivity enhancement can help people and goods travel more quickly (i.e. linked to jounrey time and journey time reliability, as well as opening new destinations and new journeys, comfort and quality service provision is relevant to public transport, e.g. detering jounreys at particular times or by certain modes (e.g. overcrowding), impact on productivity at work for commuters, safety and security , due to loss of output from workers, transport accidents occur easily. All of these issues will impact any countries' standard of living to local people (geography) , even GDP income.

Why does the direct and indirect effects of transportation have a positive impact on the economic growth and development of a country? Does it influence acccess to goods, services and
employment opportunities in any regions? Underdeveloped countries must need to consider how transport system influences their economic growth. For example, the costs of transportation and production are reduced through timely delivery and enhancing the economies of scale in the production process, when the road is often traffic joam, gas cost, time waste , air pollution cost, noise has many roads, but if one lorry drivers needs drive more than one day to day to deliver goods to another city's warehouse every day. It will bring psychological pressure in terrible, when they need long time to drive on the road. They can not sleep easily because road accident will occur easily when they need to spend long time to drive lorries on the road.

So, how to solve the long driving time on road transport problem will be one issue concerns human life welfare benefit aspect, instead of economic benefit aspect. The transport system welfare worth needs to include human life worth. It is a valuable insight into the causality (ot lack of causality) between transport and economic growth and will serve to compare to any countries‘ national level and local geographical location level both.

In special, underdeveloped countries' public transport time whether it is long or short factor, it will influence workers their going to offices to work time. If they often need spend long time to catch buses, due to traffic jam,then it will influence their efficiences to be reduced, productive number is influenced to reduce also, because traffic jam causes they often go to offices too lately.It can influence workers‘ bad emotion to work every day. So, traffic jam will bring negative relationship between low efficiency and bad emotion to the workers, because they need to spend long time to wait, public transportation tools and traffic jam also influence their working emotion. Consequently, service and working performance will be influenced to poor, because long time traffic jam problem causes their bad emotion to work. It is one critical factor in the path of more widely spread economic growth and urbanization for traffic jam problem to underdeveloped countries.

However, transport system can also influence developed countries' economy. How does it influence on environmental impacts aspect from mature stage. Its business activities must raise, dramastic expansion during this period, such as underdeveloped country, US, UK. In order to acheive long term sustainable development , new demands are being placed on transport sector, such as underground mass transit rail transport , ferry, local air frieght transport, train , e.g. Japan, Fance, US high speed prior rail. Because their developed countries , business and entertainment activities needs increase, it influences high time efficient and rapid speed public transportation tools needs are also needed in societies. These new technological public transport tools invention will impact on climate, noise, human health, land use and damage to ozene layer, acidification aspects, instead of economic beneficial aspect.

For long -term sustainable development to be achieved, the various activities within developed and underdeveloped societies must be adapted to what can be tolerated by humans and by the natural environment. Transport is an activity which affects humans and the natural environment for both the development of society as a whole as well as for the mobility for the individual. For Swedish underdeveloped country example, air pollution in Swedish urban areas has beed reduced, but in many places concentrations of certain substances deiving from transport activities are still at unacceptable levels and much more has to be done. Carbon dioxide emissions and noise are examples of environmental problems demanding further efforts. Measures to limit the exploitation of valuable natural and cultural environments to protect biological diviersity are also needed. So, if Swedish still hopes to develop its tourism industry to attract many travellers to choose to travel itself country. It needs to solve environmental problems from different modes of transport are of different dimensions, such as improving its air transport to avoid cause different problems and rail transport differs in turn from road transport.

The transport problem to Swedish may include poor technological communication information to its public and purchasers of transportation and communication services as to the environmental effects of different solutions is significant in creating the demand for environmentally sound public transport service concepts. It is therefore important that such lacking high technological communication and information system is presented in as completem accurate and clear way as a method for non-monetary comparison of the environmental public transport service system aspect.

In real, it's public tranport service system is needed to be improved and upgraded in order to let travellers feel Swedish's any rail, underground train, ferry, bus , taxi etc. different public transport travelling service can provide excellent performance to serve their travelling passengers, when they need to catch any kinds of public transport tools to go to travel. They can feel convenient and comfortable to attract them to visit Swedish to travel again. Then, its tourism industry GDP income will be raised, if Swedish government can innovate any new kinds of purchase ticket equipment to install in and public transport stations to let travelling passengers feel that they do not need to spend long time to queue to buy tickets to catch ferry, train, underground mass transit rail on stations conveniently. Because long time purchase ticket queue waiting will cause travellers feel its public service performance dissatisfaction and they will complain , even they won't choose to catch the kind of public transport, even the travellers won't choose to travel Swedish again, if they feel Swedish is one developed country, but it neglects to take care about travellers' catching public transport travelling service needs.

It is one poor or bad feeing to let travellers choose to Swedish again. Hence, Swedish needs to improve its public transport service performance in order to achieve to raise their comfortable and satisfactory catching public transport tools needs to let travellers to feel. They may include efficient land use for transportation tools, comprising issues concerning natural and cultural environment, natural resources, biological diversity and aesthetics, noise reducing, public transportation energy consumption and time consumption reducing, raising public transport service facilities performance functions and other issues concerning the model. For example, Swedish government can facilitate the public transport price conparison and journey time spending comparison information gathering enquiring machines public transportation selection method of public transportation services to let every travellers can evaluate different modes of public transport when they are staying in ferry, bus, train, underground mass transit rail, taxi stations.

A travelling family can seek its sustainable transport selection system for passenger transport tool. When they touch the enquiry machine, they can compare busm ferry, train, underground train, taxi price and journey spending time from their transportation stations to another destinations. Then, travelling passengers can compare these public transport tools ticket prices, journey spending time immediately when they touch the public transport enquiring machines in stations any time. Then, they can make the most righ choice to decide whether they ought catch which kind of public transport tool to arrive the another journey destination. It is one every attractive high technological enquiry method to help any travelling passegners to choose which kind of public transport tool, it can be the most cheap transport tool at the moment in any public transport stations. So , for developed countries innovative its public transport service performance will need future passengers' journey needs daily. Hence, they can not neglect how to improve public transport service needs to satisfy passengers to feel satisfaction, if Sweden government hopes its tourism industry can raise GDP income in long time.

● How underground train MTR can let passengers to feel catching time reducing

It has close relationship between globalization and global tranport development. How globalisation impacts on the environment via changes taking place in the transport sectors. In fact, it is not clear how the relative price changes that result from openness will affect the environental composition of economic activity. For example, some countries will produce more environmentally intensive goods, others will produce fewer. On the other hand, liberalisation will raise incomes, perhaps increasing the willingness to pay for environmental improvement. These potential income effects increased outweigh the negative scale effects with increased economic activities. When combined with the positive effects with technology transfer, the net effect on local pollutants could be positive . Hence, we need to find methods to solve the problem of raising transport economic activities and serious environmental pollution creating as the same time occurrence.

Globalisation helps to facilitate greater division of labor, and to exploit its comparative advantage more completely. In longer term, globalization also stimilates technology an dlabour transfers, and allows the dynamism that accompanies economic activities to stimulate the development of new transport technologies and short time transport processes that lead to global welfare improvement.

On shipping transport industry aspect, shipping will increase ocean pollution, when international shipping activities are increasing. Trade and shipping encourages energy use in shipping is coupled with the movement of waterborne commerce. The estimates depending on the transport goods number of at-sea or in port days much increase globally every day. The energy demand of international shipping fuel sale number and domestically assigned fuel sales number also increases for global fuel usage. Estimates of ocean going ships now consume about 2% to 3% and perhaps even as much as 4% of world fossil fuels.Hence, when global shipping energy fuel usage number increases, because global shipping trading activities number increases. It will bring the environmental pollution to ocean level increases. On air transport industry aspect, their travellers‘ catching air plans travelling needs and businesses' goods transport air delivery service needs are increasing from the requirements for high quality , fast and reliable international transport. Moreover, the networks that airline companies operate have changed often to hub-and spoke networks, many new often low -cost companies have entered the air freight market, any long time air journey is needed, e.g. Australia airline expands its one new air journey flies to UK, it needs two days flying time. It means that every flight to UK from Australia , it needs to use more fuel to fly. Then , air pollution will increase also.

On road transport industry aspect, global road transport cost and transit times, traffic jam occurrence chances also increase because when the road building number is increasing globally. So, it will cause traffic jam and long journey time spending , even fuel usage spending number is also increased. Then, accident occurrence chance is raised. Hence, global business or entertainment transport activities number increasing , it will bring much negative impact on environmental pollution, traffic jams number increases, long journey spending time increases, fuel usage number increases. Although , frequent transport activities may bring GDP income.

On transport service industy aspect, but is also brings negative influence to standard of living. It means that when transport fuel demand increases, transport activities number increases, GDP income on relative any transport activities needs industy , e.g. logistic demand needs, when lorry drivers need to drive lorries to deliver goods from one warehouse to another warehouse or supermarket or office etc. different business places on the road driving activities increase. But, it also bring air pollution , traffic noise and traffic jam etc. transport problems to road and natural environment and raises worse standard of living , bad emotion to working people or learning emotion to students , due to frequent traffic jam causes , low efficiency and productivity to workers, even student individual learning time can be reduced if they need to spend long time to wait bus, ferry, rail, underground train to go to schools , due to frequent long time traffic jam occurs on the roads to influence they can not go to schools on time often when they are catching buses to go to schools absolutely in busy transport time.

Thus, although any countries need to consider how to design their transport system, e.g. how to e.g. how to choose the right locations to build roads to let many cars can be driven available easily when the morning and evening (office and school transport busy time, e.g. 6:00 to 9:00 AM morning, 6:00 to 9:00 PM in the evening transport time usually because these two transport periods are usually , there are many students and working people need to catch any public transportation or drive cars tools to go back homes. So, enough roads number and long and not narrow road area must be needed to design in order to let enough cars be driven on the roads in the transport busy times to the countries have many big cities or have high population , such as UK, US, China, India, Hong Kong. They have many people , but drivers and cars numbers both are increasing. So, efficient road design and road number are also needed to increase in order to let drivers can transport goods to deliver, students and working people can catch any public transport tools to arrive any destinations on reads in the short time rapidly in order to avoid to spend long time transportation time and late to arrive any destinations in possible occurrence. So, any sudden traffic jam is not hoped to be caused by easy traffic accidents occurrence any time.

Hence, global efficient road transport system is needed, when global transport activities are increased, because any road logistic transport activities are increasing, they will also influence the students and working people when they also need to catch any public transport tools or drive themselves cars to go to working places or schools on the roads at the same busy transport time between 6:00 to 9:00 AM morning busy transport time and between 6:00 to 9:00 PM evening busy transport time. Because these both times will be have many students, working people , they need either go to offices or schools or go to homes. Hence, if the country had many lorry drivers need to drive their lorries to deliver goods on the roads in the transport busy morning or evening time in the same driving time on the roads. It will increase the risk to cause frequent traffic jam or traffic accident occurrence easily in possible in the country. So, any countries' governments can not neglect how to design roads and choose anywhere are the roads suitable locations to be built as well as anywhere land useful number to build road location choices in order to solve geographical traffic jams occurrence chance.

Hence, globalization of transport activities may bring geographical GDP growth, but it also bring traffic jams and traffic accidents occurrences, hearing impairment due to traffic noise, air pollution, traffic crashed, bad working emotions to workers and bad learning emotions to students, due to spending long transport time when traffic jam or traffic accidence occurs more easily.

However, transportation is an important tool if a country's progress. Rapid economic growth and increasing level of urbanization enhances a person's living standard have, it leads to a greater travel demands. Hence, governments ought not neglect have to design its roads , measure every road's length or width whether it has how many cars need to drive in morning or evening transport busy time for students, working people and delivery goods drivers of public transportation tools or private transportation tools easy driving needs in order to avoid frequent traffic jams or traffic accidents occurrences in possible.

Moreover, any governments also need to solve these issues, if they hope to develop their transport system successfully. These issues include : What mode of transportation to cost-effective in meeting a region's transportation needs to the country? How should a state department of transportation prioritize its highway delivers to maximize economic growth? What is the trade-off between additional growth in urban area and the cost of expanding transportation systems to accommodate greater growth? What effect does the expansion of transportation systems have on the need to invest in other types of transport modes? For example , the transport expansion may include the construction of additional highway segments, rail lines, runways, or additional sea, air, rail or bus terminal capacity using traditional technology; highway may include the additional of lanes to an interstate highway system; the conversion of an existing two-lane road to a four lane limited access highway, replacement or widening of bridges, and the extension of an existing road. Airport examples, include runway lengthening, apron expansion, and additional terminal gates.

On the other hand, enhancement to new transport technologies may bring efficiency of the existing highway system, examples may include intelligent highway systems, congestion pricing, intermodal freight facilities, geographic positioning systems, and instrument landing systems to mention of a few major transport innovations. So, transport policy makers need to understand the effects of these new transport mode innovations on economic development or GDP growth on transport activities growth transportation services and a more efficient use of limited land supplying scarce resources , air quality ,and noise pollution, traffic jams, long spending transport time to students, working people, entertaining people, even deliver goods lorry drivers their every day essential driving activities or catching public transportation tools needs problems. For example, the concept of intelligent highway systems needs increase trend. In simply , vehicles are being linked to each other and to traffic control devices to improve the efficiency of the total highway system. Similar types of innovations in intelligent traffic management are increasing needs for air, sea, and rail systems. The question is that whether intelligent highway systems can attribute of highways on economic development, raising on productivity of reducing highway congestion or improving pavement condition.

In fact, many developed countries' transportation system is mature. The nation has gone beyond the frontier of building, the interstate highway system and connecting most cities (markets). Tweaking the system with additional lanes and the new intelligent highway systems are useful in China, US, UK, because they have many cities. SO, road efficient traffic congestion control is needed when many students, working people, delivery goods transport people need to drive cars or catch cars on every city's roads in the transport busy time between 6:00 to 9:00 AM morning transport busy time as well as between 6:00 to 9:00 PM evening transport busy time.

However, transportation investment must be needed, if the country hoped to have good economic productivity, efficient transport service can bring good effects on the flows goods and people on roads every day when they use the country's transport system. So, any countries need to collect data, they can not be lack of enough transport information in any time that links anywhere locations of any drivers to the locations of the transport system that provide them with services in any time, e.g. every day morning and evening transport busy time, radio can report the real transport time of any roads traffic jam or traffic accident message to let drivers to listen to know whether anywhere roads are occurring traffic accidents or traffic jams or when the road traffic accident or traffic jam is solved to let the drivers can know whether when the roads can be opened to drive again. So, real time road transport message information is needed to report by radio, in order to let any drivers to know whether they ought choose to drive themselves cars on the road when they need to choose anywhere road to drive to the destination if they can know when the road has traffic accident or traffic jam occurs. They won't drive their cars on the road in the moment immediately.

On conclusion, globalization can being frequent transport economic activities. So, road , air, sea, transport service users' transport service needs are also increased. Every country ought not neglect how to innovate their transport service in order to satisfy their transport needs to achieve economic growth, efficient and short transport time spending, productivities increase, reducing air pollution, traffic noise , raisins standard of living on transport influence aspect to satisfy working people, students, entertaining people, delivery goods transport users' efficient road transport time behavioral spending aspect.

Artificial intelligent public transport how influences passenger psychology

How technology influence passenger psychology

Nowadays, robotic invention can be applied to factory manufacture, hotel, restaurant, shopping center, customer service, accounting, law document draft etc. general office tasks aspect, evem hospital surgen patient medical operation health service aspects. If future robotic non -manual driving vehicles can be invented to reach the safe auto driving mature skill stage. Any one driver begins to believe robotic, driving safe level is bette than he/she drives himself/herself car. I assume that if future robotic public transport tool drivers can replace human public transport tool drivers to drive bus, taxi, train, tram, ferry, underground train, tram , even air plane ets. different kinds of public transport tools. How non maual driving public transport tools influence our social change either to improve better ot worse? How non manual driving public transport tools influence passenger psychology, e.g. increasing any kinds of public transport tools passengers safe feeling to choose to catch any kinds of public transport tools to go to anywhere or feeling more dangerous when the passenger himself/herself chooses to sit the non manual driving public transport tool.

In past, traditional public transport tools are driven by human drivers, if one day non manual driving skills are invented to reach the most safe level, when the car owner or passenger is sitting on the non manual driving vehicle or public transport tool, the artificial intelligent driver can help the driver to control the car wheel to avoid to crash any other cars or pedestrians to o to any far places on the roads easily. The public bus does not human driver to drive the bus, artificial intelligent driver won't feel tried, when it drives the bus long time, it does not need to leave the bus to go to toilet, to go to restaurant to eat, to go to rest room for rest, because it is one (AI) machine. So, the (AI) driver won't have negative emotion to feel angry when the bus passenger complaints its service is poor when he feels dissatisfactory to the (AI) driver bus service performance.

However, human bus driver may be complainted for unpolite or rude bus service attitude. It is common human bus driver will encounter any unreasonable passenger complain in general . Hence, when non manual driving technology can be invented to reach the most safe driving skill level, whether (AI) machine driver is the most suitable to replace any public transport tool drivers, such as bus, taxi, train, underground train, ferry, tram, even air plane to drive for future passengers service need.

In fact, any public transport tool drivers may cause traffic transport accidents, due to their careless driving to crash any other vehicles or pedestrians (walling people). Consequently, any passengers may have chance to be killed by public transport tool crashing accident. So, it seems that global public transport tools are dangerous to any passengers, when they are sitting on the bus, taxi, train, tram, underground train road public transport tools, or ferry sea public transport tools, because any human public transport tool drivers will feel tried to drive any one kind of public transport tool long time, for example when the bus driver has no enough nervous to drive the bus, he wants to sleep, due to he often needs to follow night time bus timetable to drive bus long time at night. When he often want to sleep and he is driving the bus, traffic accidents will be caused easily. So, any passenger individual life is dominated by the sleeping bus driver. His bus dirving behavior is not safe to any one bus passenger when the bus passegner chooses to catch this feeling sleeping bus driver's bus to catch.

Otherwise, (AI) non manual driver must not feel tried or need sleep often. It is one automative driving mature, it can drive any kinds of public transport tools all day, because (AI) machine drivers do not need sleep, (AI) none human auto-driving driver can bring this important unique benefit to any kinds of public transport tools to compare human drivers. Instead of (AI) automatic driving tools' non need sleeping advantage, (AI) non-manual control auto-driving tools must not own sad, disappointing feeling , tried feeling, anygry emotion feeling when it needs to contact angry passengers every day. So, I mean that any traffic accident occurrence will reduce, when (AI) drivers often feel happy to drive any kinds of public transport tools. Otherwise, any human public transport drivers will be influenced to feel angry when they are complaint by angry passenger in any driving time easily. So, public transport traffic accident will be caused to occur easily. Althoug, it is not guarantee that it is obsolute none any public transport accident occurrence, due to crash to other vehicles, during the non manual driving (AI) driver drives the bus, tram, train, taxi, on the road, nut when (AI) non manual driving skill can be improved to the most safe driving level. I believe that non manual driving public transport tools ought be bring more safe to compare human public transport tools drivers to any one passenger individual life safety.

How non manual driving automated vehicle influences future mode of public transport service change? A survey distributed in the Netherlands in which respondents had to choose between conventional cars, public transportation for different travel distances and trip purposes. having collected information from 663 respondents, conducted a study on classic trip attributes (such as travel time, car owner self driving time and non manual driving public transport tool driving time as well as travel costs, car owner car fuel purchase expenditure and general non manual driving public transport tool fare comparison), attitudinal factors and socio-economic variables to understand future non manual auto driving public transport tools choices. The repor indicates that automated driving transport service which they defined as an automatically controlles door-to-door transport service provided by a vehicle with similar features to a conventional car, albeit driveless. Results suggest that travellers' mode preferences vary significantly for different travel distances and purposes. They found that conventional cars and public transportation are perceived as being the least attraction altererrnatives in relation to vehicle travel time and short -and -long distance commuting trips respectively, preference for passegner choice is between the non-manual driving auto car and non manual driving auto public transport tool.

They indicated that future passengers will consider how non-manual driving public transport tools whether they can bring trips are safer, faster and more efficient to let them to feel as well as traveling time and time cost is also another factor to influence them to choose to catch non-manual driving public transport tool, when they feel safe to arrive the destination rapidly. Then, future many passengers will be persuaded to choose to catch non-manual auto driving public transport tools in preference. So, if future all public transport service providers can let passengers to feel fares are reasonable price, when their non-manual driving public service transport tools, bus, taxi, tram, train, underground train etc. they can let them to feel safe to arrive destinations rapidly, they won't need worry about passengers number will reduce when human drivers are replaced by AI robotic drivers. In fact, when one needs to drive to arrive destination in long driving time. The car owner will feel tried, bored and he/she can not spend driving time to do his/her interesting activites in his/her car, e.g. reading, listening music, watching TV, playing electronic games from smartphone, phone talking etc. personal behaviors. So, it means that future long time trip passengers may be persuaded to catch non-manual auto driving public transport tools if they believe that this kind of new non manual auto driving pubic transport tools can provide more safe, efficient, rapid, comfortable feeling to them, when they are sitting on them.

All of these may be the main factors to influence them to choose to catch non -manual auto driving public transport tools. In general, these other factors may influence future passengers to choose to catch non manual auto driving public transport tools, they may include: whether automated vehicle would drive on populated streets better than conventional cars, whether an automated car would be comfortable entrusting the safety of a close family member, whether automated vehicle might produce fewer pollutant emissions. Because , when future non-manual auto driving vehicles are popular, many car owners will choose to buy automated vehicles to drive. So, future non manual auto driving public transport tool service providers , their competitors may be automated vehicles. If automated vehicles can let car owners to feel car prices are reasonable, they can provide safe, rapid speed, comfortable feeling to any one car owner, then he/she can sell his/her traditional car to change new automated car easily, when global many car owners begin to accept automated cars.

On conclusion, future passengers may be persuaded to choose to buy fares to catch any kinds of non manual auto driving public transportation tools. It depends on these factors, such as reasonable fares, safe feeling, efficient and rapid arriving to destinations short time journey, comfortable and clean seats facility, free personal behavior, e.g. quite reading , listening music, watching TV , free internet provision transport environment, when future any one passenger is sitting in the auto driving public transport vehicle. So, (AI) technology will have possible to influence our future social public transportation development may bring more significant new travelling experiences and it can let global passengers to feel indeed. Moreover, it will be future global public transportation service providers, they need to consider that they ought need to change their public transport tools services in order to satisfy future passengers transport needs more easily. I conclude that future global public transport service will be influenced to change non manual auto driving public transport services by future global passegner public transport service needs within 10 years. So, nowadays, any kinds of public transport service providers ought need to spend time to research how to design themselves traditional public transport service moods to change to non manual auto driving moods in order to satisfy future global passenger individual new public transport services needs successfully.

CHAPTER VI

Artificial intelligence and the future of defense or teaching choice

Nowadays, artificial intelligence (AI) is widely knowledge to be one kind of the dramatic technology. However, it is expected to continue, to have a disruptive impact on human's private and public life, so defense and security will be no exception. But how exactly will these be affected ? How will (AI) defense and security is incremental in nature? If (AI) technological machine men are applied to teach students in education aspect, is it better to my next generation learning develpment more than they are applied to war attack aspect.

To research why artificial intelligence (AI) has possible to be used to cause autonomous weapons by human. We need to understand these three aspects of relationship. They include cybersecurity and artificial intelligence and machine learning and autonomous weapon systems relationship between of them. Basic on (AI) machine can be invented to learn any new knowledge, so if (AI) machine men are taught how to attack enemy, which will be such as human soldier function. But, if (AI) machine men are taught how to learn university knowledge to teach students. Then, they will be such as human lecturer function. So, when (AI) is invented to own human mind and judgement and learning abilities, then they will be either human's enemy or human's assistant, such as university lecturer's assistant.

Firstly, we need to know what is the mean of artificial intelligence and cyber defense/offense? It means defense of critical networks: real time, pattern finding, anomaly seeking, it must utilize machine (AI) learning algorithms to efficiently, and instantaneously respond to potential network threats as well as it means human on or out of the loop. On the loop : it means anomaly detection: human notified, IT analysis, response. Out of the loop: it means anomaly detection: (AI) decides best method of response: quarantine, honey pot monitoring, hack-back. Thus, it is possible that (AI) can be used , such as autonomous cyber weapon. If (AI) is applied to make the decision best method of response to learning aspect, such as univeristy different subject knowledge. Then, it will be one good technological educational tool to teach university students.

In simplicity, (AI) can be one of scientific weapons platform or one of university teaching tool. When one day, it is invented to be applied to control war planes to fly to any countries to attack enemies or it is invented to be seemed to human to replace soldiers to bring guns or any weapons go to other countries to attack. So, it is possible that future any war defense planes, (AI) technological automatic control weapon can be replaced of human soldiers or war plane pilots to control any war defense planes to go to different enemy countries to attack them easily. It is very horror matter to threaten global human's ourselves life in the future , if (AI) automatic control war defense planes or (AI) automatic control machine soldiers were invented successfully. Otherwise, when one day, (AI) machine lecturer is invented to be applied to learn university different subjects knowledge to replace lecturers to copy lecturer's every prepared lecturer course to speak to let students to listen when they are sitting in university halls as well as the (AI) machine lecturer can make analysis and judgement response to answer every student's enquire immedicately after it had speaking all courses to students to listen in lecturer hall every time. Then, it can let human lecturer does any education job duty, e.g. research education work. So, (AI) machine lecturer will be future human lecturer's assistant in future one day.

Finally, the most serious (AI) technological invention risks are human is unknown these aspects of (AI) absolutely: They are not simple automatic systems, learning reasoning, communication of " self-aware" systems. Thus, human will face (AI) technological invention risks or threats if human invent (AI) machine man to learn how to attack enemy. Otherwise, if human invent (AI) machine man to learn how to teach univerity student. I believe that my future university students can raise learn ability and writing ability and reading ability from (AI) machine lecturer teaching more than human lecturer teaching.

1.1 Online technology and online book technology influences artificial intelligence mind development

Nowadays, online technological invention bring online book technological development. Also, artificial intelligent technological machine men had been invented to link internet to do any jobs, e.g. children can find any data from artificial intelligent machine men when the artificial intelligent machine man had been installed internet and computer function, then children can find any online books to read from the artificial intelligent machine man. Such as Japan artificial intellgent machine men had installed computer and internet function, the Japan family children can find any online books to read from the artificial intelligent machine man at Japan any families' homes conveniently. Hence, it implies that future one day, artificial intelligent machine has possible to be invented to own human's reading and/or writing abilities.

For example,online book publishing is one kind of popular internet technology. For example, Amazon publish is as a business model with many potential advantages, relative to a physical operation. It held out the potential of lower book inventing and distribution costs and reduced overhead. Consumers could find the books, they were looking for more easily and a variety book topic choices could be offered for sale. It can accept and fulfill orders from almost any domestic location with equal ease. And most purchasers made on its site would be exempt from sales tax. One Amazon strategy hand, it would have to make its returns and redress processes transparent and reliable, and offer other ways for clients to learn, as much about the book possible before buying. Future online book market development trend, such as Amazon, Barnes & Noble etc. online book shops.

Hence, online book store technology can be applied to artificial intelligent technology. Such as artificial intelligent machine men can apply computer technology to learn the abilities of reading and/or writing any books either on paper or on computer. Hence, it is possible that artificial intelligent machine men will have similar human's writing and/or reading books ability when they own human's mind ability. However, it bring this questions: Can artificial intelligent machine men own human's mind abilities? If they own human's mind abilities, is it mean that they can write and/or read any books? Can artificial intelligent machine men own human's mind abilities to create to write any books? Can artificial intelligent machine men own human's mind abilities to read and make any judgements or decisions more accurate than human's judgements or decisions? To answer these questions? I shall indicate that online book reading and writing technology can be applied to artificial intelligent machine men reading and writing technology. Because they are similiar computer mind technological development. So, I believe that future artificial intelligence machine men can be invented to own similar human's reading and writing's mind abilities in future one day.

I believe artificial intelligence and online technological reading abilities are very similiar. Nowadays, computer can be invented to attempt to read and write any books by human. Why can not artificial intelligent machine men replace computer to read and write any books? Artificial intelligent machine men can replace human to attempt to write or/and read books, due to artificial intelligent machine men had invented to own human mind to do some jobs and their mind had been invented to be similiar to human behavioral abilities to do these behaviors, e.g. cooking, driving, playing games, singing songs, speaking, listening, frighting etc. different human's abilities. So, it seems that artificial intelligent will be possible to be invented to own human's mind abilities to do any writing or reading behaviors or functions.

1.2 Prediction of artificial intelligence reading and writing abilities

development

What is future trend of artificial intelligence reading and writing abilities development? To answer this question, we need to know what benefits of artificial intelligent machine men can attribute to human's needs when they can own any human's mind to read or/and write any books.

I shall indicate e-books reading and writing example, if artificial intelligent machine men can be invented to own human's mind to write and/or read e-books on computer. Then, it brings this question: Can artificial intelligent machine men assist human to learn to do judgement to solve any challenges?

I believe that when artificial intelligent machine men can be invented to own human mind to write or/and read any books, then they will own human's mind ability to make judgement to solve any challenges more accurately, even their decisions can be more accurate to compare to human's decisions. So, artificial intelligent machine mens' writing and reading ability is the main factor to cause their mind to do any judgement in order to make any decisions more accurately. Consequently, in future one day, artificial intelligent machine mens‘ writing and reading ability will be invented to similar human's reading and writing abilities as well as their minds can also be invented to similar human's minds as well as their judgement abilities can be invented to similar to human's judgement abilities to make any decisions more accurate.

1.3 The influences when AI is invented to own human's mind and judgement abilities

Finally, I shall discuss what are the influences when AI is invented to own human's mind and judgement abilities in our future job market. The achievement of artificial intelligent (AI) machine men achievement requirement of owning human's mind and judgement abilities which requires extensive manual labor, and by augmenting the calling process with machine learning, the process where speed and accuracy are needed to close to human's mind and judgement abilities. Expert human race callers now have better information at artificial intelligent machine men at their fingertips faster.

Hence, if the above those requirements are achieved to satisfy artificial intelligent machine men ind and judgement abilities demand to close or exceed humans' mind and judgement abilities. Then, I believe that future human's some simple jobs must be replaced by (AI) machine men. Even, human's some professonal jobs, e.g. lawyer, accountant, administator, typing etc. professional skillful jobs, which will be either replaced or will be assisted by (AI) machine men. For example, (AI) machine men learn how to type english or other language words to do typing job ; they can learn how to apply accounting knowledge to record any firm's income and expenditure record of accounting job; they can also learn how to assist architects to design any architectural building drawing plans to do architect jobs; they can learn how to analyze any court evidences to judge any criminal or civil cases and assist lawyers to give legal advices to achieve more reasonable judgement for any legal cases; they can also learn how to assist firm's managers or administrators to manage any organization teams efficiently.

Consequently, when (AI) machine men can be invented to achieve to exceed human's mind and judgement abilities level. Then, I believe that they can do instead of human' simple jobs, which can do even human's more difficult and more judgement requirement of professional skillful jobs. So, (AI) machine men must need to achieve to do any jobs, they are same, even exceed to human professionals' abilities. Then, it will cause a lot of human's jobs to be disappeared or some human's jobs will be replaced by owning judgement and mind abilities of (AI) machine men to do.

Hence, future many human's jobs will be replaced by technological labors. Employers choose to buy (AI) machine men to replace human labors. The reasons include (AI) machine men have none unhappy, angry emotin to influence their low efficiencies and low productivities. Their judgement and mind abilities can exceed human's abilities or do any jobs to compare better performance to human's abilities. Consequently, different occupation labors need to prepare to learn how to co-operate with (AI) machine men to let future employers feel (AI) machine men will be human's assistant to assist human to do jobs efficiently when human and (AI) machine men work together. It aims to avoid future employers feel (AI) machine men's judgement and mind abilities can exceed any low knowledgeable and skilful occupation labors, even high knowledge and skilful occupation labors. It means that (AI) machine men are only labors' assistant if (AI) machine mens' judgement and mind abilities are below under to human labors' judgement and mind abilities.

Consequently, to avoid (AI) machine men can replace human to do any simple or complex jobs to cause any future any occupation labors' competitiors. I recommend that it is right time labors ought prepare to learn different skills. So, every individual labor does not only concentrate on one kind of skill. Because supposing one kind of the occupation labor's job duties are replaced by (AI) machine men. If the employee had owned more than one kind of occupation skill. Then, I believe that who can avoid the unemployment threat more easier than the employee only owned one kind of occupation skill, when (AI) machine men had invented to own human's mind and judgement abilities in future one day.

Why does AI machine lecturer can raise education quality

When (AI) machine men can own human reading and writing and judgement and analytical abilities, then they can replace university lecturers to teach students to raise students' learning abilities absolutely. Then, it bring this question: Why does I machine lecturer can raise education quality? Why do universities prefer to apply (AI) machine lecturer to teach teachers more than human lectuer in university lecturer hall learning environment? Will (AI) university lecturers replace human lecturers to teach students to learn at university lecturing halls popularly? Can (AI) university lecturers replace university human lecturers to teach students more easily and it can let students feel more easily to learn when they are listening what (AI) university lecturers are teaching to them every time university lecture.

In university today, nearly all students need to attend university lecturing hall to listen their lecturer's teaching in every time course. However, many students do not feel interesting to attend university halls to listen human lecturer's teaching. The reasons include, they are busy, so no time to attend lecturer's hall to listen lecturer's teaching; or they feel bore to listen their lecturer's teaching; they feel difficulty to learn; they have confidence to exam and do their assignments, so they feel that they do not need to go to lecturing halls to listen their human lecturer's teaching. However, if one day, (AI) machine lecturers are invented to teach university students to learn and solve their learning difficulties. Can it raise student individual learning interest, due to (AI) machine lecturers' education quality is better than human lecturers‘ education quality?

What will influence to university students if (AI) machine lecturer can invented to replace human lecture? The influences will include such as below:

First reason: the only way is going to be useful to university lecturers are if all (AI) machine lecturers are well-informed and fully supported to assist human lectuers to teach whose students to let them to listen whose teaching absolutely. So, human lecturers can concentrate on doing any education research and data gathering jobs to prepare for (AI) machine lecturers to help them to explain human lecturers' every time prepared course contents more efficiently. So, (AI) machine lectuers can help human lecturers to share whose teaching time in lecturing halls. Human lecturers‘ can spend whose hall lecturing time to do whose educational research or other educational gathering jobs absolutely.

The second reason, the human lecturer (Human capital) has ability and efficiency of concentrating on education data gatehering research jobs to prepare to write whose books. When (AI) machine lecturer replace the human lecturer to spend time to attend lecturing hall to teach students. Fo long term, the human lecturer can raise education productivity growth and education quality raising, due to who only concentrate on searching or gathering data to prepare to write whose books to raise their education level.

In macro and micro economic view, the well (AI) machine lecturer educated labor (human capital) is often replaced to human lecturer as one of the critical factors to influence rapid education productivities and educational quality growth to the Asia developing countries' any regions or cities. Because any of these Asia developing countries, such as China, Korea, Philippines etc. countries which need have well educated and knowledgeable lecturer labors to raise any universities' educational productivities and educational qualities growth. So (AI) assistant lecturer factors which ought have close relationship to cause the good or bad future student learning effectiveness and education or learning qualities raising in these any one of Asia developing countries.

The third reason, for the big population of student growth number example, China's student growth rate is larger than school growth rate. If China expect every students have enough chance to study in schools, but university human lectuer numbers are not enough to supply to universities to teach their students. I believe that (AI) machine lecturer is only one kind of teaching method to solve these big population countries' university lectuer number shortage challenge.

In conclusion, in long term, (AI) machine lecturers can solve university human lecturer shortage challenge as well as they can attract many students to attend lecturing halls and human lecturers can raise education quality when they can concentrate on searching or gathering data to prepare their education career, when (AI) machine lectuers replace them to spend time to attend univesity halls to teach students in every university lecturing time.

Future AI machine education market

I believe that when AI (artificial intelligent machine men) which can invented to own to similar to human mind, learning, language, analytical, judgement abilites. Then, which can be applied to any education market service industy. (AI) potential education market service industy includes such as below:

● (AI) university lecture assistant

Future (AI) machine men can assist univerity lectuers to attend university halls to attempt to teach university students for different subjects, e.g. english, math, economic, math, engineering, art, architect etc. different subjects. It depends on the human lectuter who prepares to spend time to teach the (AI) machine lecturer to remember whose teaching subject.

For example, the economic lecturer spend one year time to teach the (AI) machine lecturer to learn all economic knowledge. Then, the (AI) machine lecturer can use its machine brain to remember all the human lecturer's economic concepts and prepared teaching economic contents within the one year. Hence, after one year the (AI) machine lecturer can remember all the human lecturer's economic concepts and economic theories and economic contents to prepare to attend university lecturing halls to teach all first year undergraduated first year economic students confidently. It means that the human lecturer's job duties will change to teach (AI) machine lecturer to learn whose economic knowledge to prepare to let the (AI) machine lecturer to replace whom to teach whose university students; so the human lectuer can spend more time to do other research job for whose university education development. Hence, the (AI) machine lecturer can share the human lecturer teaching job as well as the human lectuer can concentrate on spending time to do whose research jobs for whose university education development. This is one both win strategy to university and the lecturer if (AI) machine lecturer is invented to assist future university lecturer's teaching jobs.

- (AI) secondary and primary teacher assistant

In the future (AI) technolgical development, instead of (AI) machine men can be applied to university education aspect. Future (AI) machine men can also be applied to secondary and primary teaching aspect. For example, primary and secondary schools do not need attend classroom to teach students. (AI) machine teachers can replace them to attempt to do teaching job. They only need to spend one year time to prepare to teach (AI) machine teacher to learn how to apply their teaching skill concern their subjects who need to teach to their students, e.g. english language writing and reading and spelling skill, sing song skill, drawing picture skill, calculation skill etc. different studying skill. Then, the (AI) primary or secondary machine teacher can apply the primary or sendary human teacher skills to attempt yo teach whose students. Hence, the primary and secondary human teacher whose duties will change to learn how to teach whose teaching skills to let the (AI) primary or seondary machine lecturer to remember how to apply human skills to teach whose students for different subjects, such as, english writing and reading and spelling language skills, singing songs language skills, math calculation skills etc. Hence, future primary or secondary school teachers who responsibilities will change to learn how to teach (AI) machine teacher teaching skills to prepare to replace them to teach their students in classroom.

- (AI) scientific research assistant

Future (AI) machine men can be applied to science research aspect, instead of school education job. For example, (AI) machine men can be any scientist's assistant, e.g. space scientist, earth or ocean scientist, human or animal behavioral psychological scientist, climate scientist, chemical scientist, drug scientist etc. How can (AI) machine men can be any kind of scientist to assist scientists to do research jobs ? I shall indiate such as below:

For space science example, the (AI) machine space scientist can assist human space scientist to gather space data to assist space scientist to research any undiscovered material to cause our earth, even space. Hence, the space scientist only need to teach the (AI) machine scientist to learn how to help them to apply space technological tools to gather data and then enter all data to computer to record, even the (AI) machine scientist can store all space data discovered record to their machine brain every day. Hence, the human space scientist does not need to spend much time to do gathering data job. The (AI) machine space scientist can help whom to do these space data gathering job, then the human space scientist can concentrate on spendin time to do space research job in whose space science laboratory every day.

For earth science example, the (AI) machine earth scientist can help the earth scientist to go to anywhere to gather earth or ocean natural activity data in our earth every day. Then, the earth scientist only need sit in whose earth laboratory to wait the (AI) machine earth scientist to come to whose laboratory to give whose gathering every day earth or ocean natural activity data to do future research job. Hence, the earth scientist does not need to leave whose laboratory to do any data gathing jobs concern earth or ocean natural activities. The (AI) machine earth or ocean scientist had helped him/her to go to our earth or ocean anywhere to do any earth or ocean activities data gathering jobs every day. Hence, the earth or ocean scientist can concentrate on spending whose time to do any research jobs in laboratory. It means that the (AI) machine earch or ocean scientist had replaced whom to do all outdoor original gathering data jobs.

For these human or animal behavioral psychological scientist, climate scientist, chemical or drug scientist, scientist all examples, the (AI) machine human or animal behavioral psychological scientist can help them to do any data gathering job, e.g. the (AI) machine scientist can learn how to help human or animal behavioral psychological scientist to contact human or animal to observe their daily activities and record all their activities data to transfer all these daily activites data to let the human or animal behavioral psychological scientist to do psychological researching analysis only. The (AI) machine climate scientist can help the human climate scientist to arrive anywhere to observe climate changes and record climate changes daily. Then, the human climate scientist only need to wait the (AI) machine climate scientist's gathering climate change data record from whose machine brain to do climate changing predict research job in climate laboratory every day. The (AI) chemical or drug machine scientist can help the drug or chemical scientist to gather data of new drug or chemical from internet channel every day. So, the human chemical or drug scientist only need to do researching job after the (AI) machine scientist transfers all daily chemical or drug information to let them to know from internet channel. It means that the chemical or drug human scientist does not need to spend much time to gather drug or chemical new data development trend from internet. The (AI) machine chemical or drug scientist had helped them to do data gathering job every day.

Consequently, future (AI) machine men can do education and research aspects of jobs duties and their role are only human scientists or primary or secondary teachers or university lecturers whose assistants either to share scientist's data gathering job or share teachers or lecturers' teaching job.

CHAPTER VII

How technological innovation may influence human behavioral change

Human Behavioral network job brings social economic benefits

What does human network job mean ? Why may human network job be popular? Why human network job behavior may influence economy ? Nowadays internet is popular to use. We can apply internet to find data , search any new things, even earn money. Why does internet may become huma network job source. For example, e-publish may be one kind of new human network job. Any authors may apply internet channel to help them to sell electronic or paper books from e-publisher web store. They may apply facebook, you tub etc. any online channel to promote themselves new books to let new readers to know whether when they may buy themselves favourable new topic books to read from electronic publisher web store.

Thus, future electronic publisher industry may help any authors to build internet network platform to help them to sell and promote ot advertise their any one new electronic or paper book topic to let global any one reader to choose to buy their any new topic books from electronic publisher web store easily and conveniently. However, it implies that electronic network platform author may be one kind of future new human network job in our societies.

How electronic network platform author job may bring economy benefit in macro economy view? A person can have few friends, contacts and still be very influential if these few friends and contacts are themselves highly influential, e.g. one author must not need to know any one reader in global society. When they like to choose any electronic books from electronic internet network platform. They may become the author's any one topic book buyer, when they feel the author's any one topic book is fun and attract they make decision to buth the strange author whose the topic book from electronic book publisher's platform web store conventiently in short time. Although, they are strangers, they do not know themselves , but the reader can understand what it way that made Google from writing platofrm to create new creative mind and typing network job method to replace traditional hand writing book method for global authors. It will be one kind of new human network writing job.

Hence, global any one reader can apply an innovative search engine , such as google.com to find whether whom author personal new topic books are value to read from internet.

Then, the electroniuc publisher's web store may be new book store platform sale network to help the author to sell many electronic or paper books from electronic network platform

in short time. So, internet may be future new network plaform to help global any one author to create network writing job absolutely. Furthermore, internet may be popular social media

to help any one author to build goold relationship between his/her readers. It is one kind of new network, human network job. New authors do not need to buy many paper books to prepare to put in any one book shop warehouse. Their every book can print on demand to reduce out of book stock in any one book shop. They may choose to sell either electronic books or paper books both from any one book publisher web store. So, electronic network platform may be one kind of good writing channel to help human authors to create income and it can also help authors to bring new creative mind and new topic fun content books to let readers to know and buy to read from electronic publisher network platform.

Why does human behavior may be one kind of new human network job to bring global economic advantages. ALthough, it may be free income or without inocme, but the person does the network behavior, his/her behavior may be bring advantages to influence many other people's health. For this case, when a worker in a coffee shop in an airport gets a vaccination aganinst the flu, it does not only helps him or her stay healthy, but also helps the many travellers who might otherwise have been inflected if that workers caught the flu. So, the externality , the result implies the vaccination of even a part of a community conveys benefits to the whole community. For example, governments pay special attention to the vaccinations of school children, teachers, health mothers, and the elderly, categories of people particularly susceptible not only to catching, but also to transmitting a disease.

It is not accidential that governments are heavily involved with vaccination . When there are externalities, free market, fail to persuade individual incentives with society's their the worker's decision of whether to get a vaccine ends up attracting whether other people get sick. The workers might not fully take all these other people's potential suffering into account when making her or his vaccination decision.

As Stanford University does many suggestions, understand this and tries to help them make the right decisions and so providers free flu vaccines for its staff and students.

Small pockets of unvaccinated individuals can allow a disease to gain a spread more widely well-being. For example, parent weighing the costs and benefits of a vaccine for their child is not always thinking of the consequences of that vaccination to other people. THese are markets in which subsidizing or regulating behavior can make everyone better off. Because the reason for requiring that a child be vaccinated before enrolling in school is not just to protect that child, because each child's vaccination affects others via potential contagions.

Robots take our jobs behavioral and economy influences

Robot job behavior brings economy influences

If one day robots can replace human to do simple, even complex jobs. They will bring what influences to our global societial economy.The popular economic refrain declares that the

global middle class is dying and robots will soon take our jobs, e.g. shopping center customer service jobs, library service jobs, cinema ticket sale jobs, restaurant kitchen cooker jobs,

even, bus drivers, taxi drivers etc. public transport driving jobs, accountant, doctors etc. professional jobs. Whether it is beautiful or petty matter if our future societies have many human jobs can be replaced to do from robots. Businessman must may reduce to employ employees and reduce to pay salary or wage, when robots can be replaced to do their employees tasks. But, societies must bring unemployement rate rises , due to societies will have many people loss jobs when their employers choose to buy robots to serve their clients or do any office tasks or customer service or cleaning etc. tasks.

In micro economy view, employers may save money in long term, but in macro economy view, it will cause unemployment ratio rises , even crime rate rises when there are many people lose

jobs in societies. These models of doom, though, fail to account for the hundreds of businesses riding the waves of change in their industries when robots may be invented to replace human to do many simple , even complex tasks in our future societies.

WE may image that one small factory needs to manufacture fishes canes to sell to supermarket, the small , cheaper stuff and higher margin parts of the fishes manufacture industry. Before, this factory needs to employe many human factory workers need to help every fresh customer makeing the perfect fishing gear, designed for performance, durability, and cost in order to achieve to manufacture every fish cane in whole fished processing manufacturing stages. Every worker needs to spend about 15 to twenty minutes to finish every fish cane , till to delivery to any supermarket to sell. If this fish canes manufacturing factory can apply manufacturing robots to help them to finish any one working tasks , every robot can only spend five minutes to finish whole fresh fish cane manufacturing process. Thus, every robot can

help this factory save 10 to 15 minutes time to finsh every fish cane manufacturing process. IN fact, time is money, because when every robot can help this factory to reduce 10 to 15 minutes time to compare human worker. Then, this factory can finish about 20 fish canes in one hour if it can use robot to help it to manufacture fish canes. Otherwise, if this factory still use human workers to help it to manufacture fish canes, then it can finsh about 3 to 4 fish canes in one hour. SO, the manufacturing efficiency ensures that robots must help this fish manufacturing factory to raise fish canes number more than human workers. So, in robotic behavioral economy view, manufacturing robots must help this fish canes manufacturing factory to raise fish canes manufacturing number and deliver increasing number to supermarkets to prepare to sell every day. Robots can help this fish canes manufacturing factory bring manufacturing time saving, rising manufacturing efficiency, improving performance and reducing wages expenditure long time advantages in micro economy view. However, manufacturing robots can also bring disadvanages to society, e.g. increasing unemployment ratio, increasing crime rate,

this factory workers will lose jobs and income, they need earn social welfare from government and increasing government finance pressure in short time, even long time in macro economic view.

Stanford University graduate program in economics, Scott lecturer explained that "in demand and supply economic theory for robots supply and demand case, robots supply number increasing may influence human workers demand number decrease. It sometimes calls " the efficient frontier".

No specific human beings were mentioned in any of economics classes. As robots supply and demand in market case, They (robots) may be purely theoretical " agents" who reached to the most reasonable sale prices in order to persuade any one businessman buyer to make manufacturing robot buying decision whether robots can help him / her to bring how much saving time , saving money, saving cost, improving performance, efficiency economic benefit before he/she plans to reduce workers number when he/she decides to apply robots to replace human workers in his/her factory or office or any service department, e.g. cinema ticket sale service, shopping center customer service, shopping center cleaning , supermarket customer service etc. service or sale tasks. When robots can replace human to do any one of these tasks in any organizations. So, robots may be human worker agents who reached to prices the way robots would react to a software command. There was nothing that explained why some people thrived and others did n't or why truly brilliant, hardworking people could fail when much lazier folks succeeded." Having been admitted to the Stanford University graduate program in economics, Scott lecturer hoped to get his answers there.

How robots influence our future social changing? Using the right technology can be a boon to your business in this economy. For internet example, it is easier than ever to find well-matched customers all around the world, to stay in contact with them, and to more quickly design the products they want. If you focus solely on being cutting -edge, though you risk letting the technology

take over what should be very robust relationships with your customers , employees, and colleagues. IN nowaddays society, technoligical advances and cutomation, personal

relationships in business are more crucial than ever. I mean that robots can not replace human to serve clients to let them to feel more comfortable and passion more easily. For shoe shop case example, if the shoe shop apply one robot to serve its clients to replace human shoe salesperson to serve its shoe customers. Robots ensure that they can not persuade every shoe potential buyer to make shoe buying decision more easily when robots need to contact every shoe potential buyer. The reason is simple, because robots can not touch any one shoe buyer individual emotion very easier.

If the shoe buyer needs the robots to help him/her to choose any right shoe styles when he/she can not feel himself / herself can make the most

right shoe style choice decision. The robots can not replace human shoe salesperson to make shoe style choice judgement more easily. They must need longer time to analyze whether which shoe style may be the most suitable to the shoe buyer. Otherwise, human shoe salesperson may attempt to make the most right shoe style choice decision to help any one shoe buyer to chooce the most right style shoe because he/she owns shoe style sale experience, shoe style knowledge, the most important reason is that they can feel every shoe customer individual emotion to touch whether he/she will feel comfortable or happy when they attempt to help every shoe customer to seek the most right shoe style in every shoe customer whole shoe searching processing. Othwerwise, serving robots are only one machine, they can not touch or feel every shoe customer individual emotion whether he/she feel comfortable or unhappy or happy when they need to contact them in whole shoe searching processing. Hence, I believe that some tasks robots can
not repalce human staff to do very easily. Otherwise, robots may bring disadvanatges to let any one businessman to loss his/her customers, due to robots can not touch every customer
emotion to compare human staff in service tasks more easily. Robots serving customer behaviors may cause money lose and customers number lose to the shop in micro economic view.

Intellectual human economic behaviors

What does intellectual human economic behaviors mean ? I believe that when we choose or decide to do intellectual behaviors, then our societies will be influenced to bring economic growth in consequence.I shall attempt to indicate pollution case to explain how and why eithet our intellectual or foolish behaviors may bring economic growth or recession in consequence as below:

On one hand, for air pollution social case aspect example, if we only consider to buy cars to drive for working aimr or holiday leisure aim. Then, our societies air will be polluted. Our health will be influenced to bad. Our car driving behaviors may cause global environment air pollution serously. In long tiem, global air pollution will bring our bodies health to be bad. Although, ourselves car driving behaviors may bring our driving travelling leisure enjoyment and comfortable feeling in short time, also we so not need to pay public transport fare often, but we need to compensate ourselves health economic intangible loss due to air pollution , when cars number increases, dirty air will cause ouselves health to become bad.

In the result, we will need to pay more medical expenditure when we are old age, due to ourselves bodies will become bad, due to we breathe global dirty air every day, due to ourselves cars pollute air in long time, e.g. 10 to 20 years, even 30 more without limited air pollution environment. So, driving cars behavior may be one kind of human foolish behavior and our foolish behavior may bring ourselves future long time medical expenditure absolutely.

One the other hand, water pollution social aspect, if we often keep much rubblish to pollute sea, oil exploration porcessing pollute ocean , ships gas pollute ocaen, then fishes will eat polluted food and drive dirty water, due to global ocean is polluted.

In fact, because human only to conside how to buy boats to carry on leisure enjoyment activities, or catch cruises to travel on the sea. Also, oil manufacturers only consider researching anywhere to find new oil exploration places to manufacture oil product, when their oil exploration processes pollute ocarn . Consequently, global fishes drink polluted warer or eat polluted food. They will have poison. SO, human will have high chance to eat poison polluted fishes, due to fishes are poison or are polluted. So, human is doing foolish activities, we only hope to find oil exploration places to pollute ocean or we only spend money to buy ticket to catch ships to travel anywhere in global ocean. All of these human foolish behaviors will bring pollution to global ocean. On consequently, we will need to compensate to eat polluted or dirty or poision fishes, ourselves bodies health will be bad. In long time, we need have high chance to pay medical expenditure when we are old. So, pollution case may be one good example to explain how and why human foolish behavior may influence ourselves future need to compensate serious medical loss.

All of these human foolish behavior will bring pollution to global ocean. On consequently, we will need to compensate to eat polluted or dirty or poison fished , ourselves bodies health will be bad. In long time, we will have high chance to pay medical expenditure, when we are old. So, pollution case may be one good example to explain how and why human ourselves intellectual or foolish behaviors may influence future long time economic loss or economic growth or recession in micro and micro economic view.

On another water pollution aspect hand, if we often keep rubbish to sea, oil exploration processing pollutes ocean and ships' gas pollute ocean, then fishes will eat polluted food and drink dirty water, due to fishes will eat polluted food and drink dirty sea water because the global ocean is polluted seriously.

In fact, because human only consider how to buy boats to carry on any leisure water activities, or catches cruises to travel on the sea. Also, oil manufacturers only consider any where to find oil exploratin places to manufacture oil products from ocean, when their pol exploration processes can plooute ocean. Consequently, global fishes drink polluted water or eat direty food. They will have poison. So, human will have high chance to eat poison fishes.

Otherwise, such as pollutin case, it can infuence inflation or deflation. Consequently, the reason indicates supply and demand theory. If air pollution is serious, then we will consider health issue, global cars demand number may be influenced to reduce, when global cars number demand will reduce, global car prices and supply number will need to change to fall down in order to attract or persuade global car consumers choose to make car purchase decision.

Hence, global car manufacture number and car price will be influenced to reduce, due to global air pollution issue. Consequently, deflation will occur because when the country citizen usually does not spend much extra saving money to buy car expensive goods. Money value will be low. Otherwise, if global cair pollution is not serious, human considers to buy cars to enjoy driving leisure lives. So, global car demand is influenced to increase , also global car price will also influenced to increase.

Consequently, gobal human will choose to buy cars to drive. Due to we accept to spend extra saving to buy expensive car goods. Car sale price and supply may be influenced to rise up. Money value is influenced to reduce. Inflation may be influenced, due to global car consumers number increases, we would not have extra money to spend easily. Car expensive goods expenditure influences our spending habit to avoid to make car purchase decision more easily. So, human intellectual or foolish activities may bring inflation or deflation consequency in possible indirectly in macro economic view.

On conclusion, above pollution case explain that how and why human intellectual or foolish economic behaviors may bring inflation or deflation consequency as wll as economic growth or recession consequency as well as any goods demand and supply increasing or decreasing consequency. It implies that human behavior may have indirect relationship to influence any goods demand and supply number to either increase or decrease result as well as any goods price will be influenced to increase or decrease in micro and macro economic view.

The relationship between social change and human behavior

Why does economic changes may influence human individual behavioral change? I shall attempt to indicate shopping behavior and staying at home behavior to explain their case and effect relationsip as below:
Human behavior can be influenced by economic change or economic change can be influenced by human behavior? Why does recession may influence consumers reduce shopping desire? In social recession suitation, it is possible that many people lose jobs suddenly, due to businessmen lose many customers. They need to make decision to reduce employees number in order to continue to keep businesses. Consequently, many firms (organizations) their employees may lose jobs. When they have much time, due to lose jobs, they will feel to avoid to spend too much time and money to go to shopping often. Many losing jobs people, they will often stay at homes. So, they will reduce time to go to shopping, then non essential products won't their preferable choice purchase products. Hence, recession will change many losing jobs people their shopping or consumption desires to avoid to buy non essential products often . Usually when economic boom, many people have jobs to do because consumers number must increase when many people have jobs to do. Then, many people can accept to spend money to buy non essential products often. Many people feel spend time to go to shopping can satisfy their purchase of any kinds of new products useful psychology or desire. So, recession is one good example to explain it can influence many people do not like often to leave homes to go to shopping easily. Many people like to stay at homes, becaue they feel worry about spending too much shopping time when they leave homes. Their staying home time is one good negative shopping behavior example. So, economic change may influence human individual behavior changes , they have direct cause and efect relationship in behavioral economic view.
May human behavior influence economic change? Is it possible that human behavior may bring the country social economic change in macro economic or micro behavioral economic view ? I shall indicate publishing industry example. Do you feel that if there are many students feel learning is very important when they read many books or many of students feel interesting to read or they have reading new books in habit, then it is possible that the country will have many students like to spend time to go to any book shops to choose the books, they feel that they can help they learn new knowledge. Then the country will increase students number, they often spend time to

visit any one book shop every week. Their visiting book shops behavior which may become their habits. So, the country will increase students number, they often spend time to visit book shops. Also, it implies that visiting book shops behaviors may be their behavioral habits.

So, when the country has many students often spend time to visit book shops , their visiting book shops behaviors may help any one book shop to raise books sale chance. So, the country's student individual often visiting book shop behaviors, their habitual visiting book shops behaviors must may assist help any one book shop to increase books sale number absolutely.

Consequently, any one book shop , its books sale bumber must be influenced to increase to increase because the country will have many students like or feel need visit book shops habit in order to choose any suitable books to buy to read at home in order to raise themselves learning effort. When the country has many bok shops often have many students visit their book shops, then their books sale number may be influenced to increase. It explain why student individual visiting book shop behavior may help any one book shop sale number increases also.

How human productive behavior may influence economic development

May any country which citizen behavior assist themselves country development? It is one cause and effect economic question. I mean that if the country itself citicen can not concentrate mind or energy to choose to do one kind of industry in order to let themselves country can bring the most benefit, then whether the counry itself economy can bring the most serious economic benefit. I shall attempt to indicate these countries themselves indistry choice to explain whether these countries themselves citizen productive behavior may help themselves countries to achieve the largest economic benefits. I shall indicate as below:

New Zealand farmer individual wine productive behavior

For New Zealand country example, this country concerns itself effort is foucs on farming agricultural aspect. So, this country has many farmers concentrate on farming agricultural aspect. May New Zealanders choose to spend time to produce different kinds of wines, e.g. wine or red grape wine is for the people are eating meat, or they are eating dinner.

When these New Zealanders their behaviors choose to do farming or agriculture to grow and produce different kinds of taste of white or red grape wine drinking products job. Themselves grape agriculture behavior will influence these New Zealanders themselves, they can learn how to improve different kinds of grape wine drinking products in order to achieve every kinds of white or read grape wines taste improving aim during their white or red grape producing process.

Why can New Zealander every individual white or read grape wine producers improve their white or read grape wine taste more easily? In behavioral economic view, it can explain that why any one New Zealander white or read grape wine producer can be encouraged or excited or persuaded to concentrate nervous and energy and effort to learn how to improve their white or red grape wine products easily.

In fact, New Zealand is one agricultural food export country. It has good natural environment resource , e.g. land, seed to provide any one farmer to produce themselves any kinds of agricultrual food products, e.g. fruit, or wine food products. Because New Zealanders know themselves country has enough natural resource . So, in common, many New Zealanders choose to attempt to do farming agricultural jobs in order to export themselves any kinds of fruit or meat or wine products to overseas or sell to domestic in order to earn profit.

So, when these New Zealand farmers number has been increasing every year. This country farmers will feel themsleves competition between this New Zealand farmers themselves are serious due to they may feel New Zealanders choose to do agriculture businesses in order to export themselves different kinds of farming food to overseas or sell to local to earn profit.

Hence, when many New Zealand farmers feel that farmers number has been increasing every year. They will feel themselves competition is serious. They must need to spend much time and nervous and effort to research what method is the best how to produce the best taste of white or red grape wine products in order to let local or overseas wine buyers to choose to buy his/her producing white or read grpae products to drink.

Hence, in competition psychological view, may influence many New Zealand white or reaad wine producers had been beginning to change their learning behavior on researching what method is the best in order to produce the best quality of taste red or white wine products to sell in order to attract overseas or local white or read grape wine drinkers to choose to buy his/her wine products. Their behavior will focus on learning how to raising or improving white or read grape wine taste method more than only focus on producing a large number white or red grape wine products. They believe wine quality is more important to compare wine producing number. So, New Zealand wine producers themselves wine producers behaviors have been changing on concentrating on researching wine quality method aspect more then wine producing number aspect in behavioral economic view.

America high technological productive behavior

For America example, US is one high technological country, it owns many high technological knowledge talent inventors, e.g. computer science inventors. Hence, US must attract many diferent countries owning high technological computer inventors choose to go to US to develop their computer science profession career. Also, it seems that when many computer science inventors or professions choose to go to US to develop themselves computer science new career. In behavioral economic view, due to their leaving themselves countries choice, which may bring influence themselve country job behaviors need to be changed. They must need to adapt US new live. Because they will forgive their past computer science job. These computer science professionals need to spend time to adapt US new lives. They " past computer science job behaviors" will need to be changed to their new US any computer employer's new computer science job model.

Because their traditional computer science jobs needed to be forgot in their themselves countries. They will feel their old computer science job knowledge and behavior needed to change in order to let their US any one new of computer company employer feels satisfactory to accept their new working behavior in any one US computer organization.

So, on the other hand, many US computer company employer will feel that they must need time to accept any one new overseas computer science professions their working behaviors, their working attitude daily, because these foreign comouter science professional, their past computer working behaviors and working attitude must be different to US domestic computer science professions.

In behavioral economic view, these overseas computer science professions, their working behaviors and attitude must be needed to change in order to adapt any one US new computer company itself domestic or local computer science professional stafs themselves daily working behaviors and attitude because these overseas and local computer science professionals must need to team work together.

In behavioral economic view, it is only one way that foreign computer science professionals must need to change themselves past country traditiona daily working behaviors and attitude in order to cooperate with these US local computer science professionals in teams more easily. Consequently, if these foreign compute science professionals can change their past working behaviors and attitude to let any one US local computer science professional feels to cooperate with them easily in short time. Then, the US computer company itself whole computer professional teams themselves efficiencies will be influenced to raised or improved by the changing past working attitude and working behaviors of these foreign computer science professionals. So, in behavioral economic view, only if US any one computer company hopes itself computer teams themselves efficiency can be raised or improved when it decides to employ foreign computer science professionals and US domestic computer science professionals. They need to work in teams together. They must need to let these foreign computer science professionals to know how to change their working behaviors and attitude to let their domestic computer science professionals feel easy to work together. Then, the US computer company itself whole team efficiency must be rasied or improved easily in short time.

- China share market investing behavior

For China share market example, economic development depends on financial market. Because if many Chinese have interest to invest to carry on shares buying and selling activities in orde to learn how to earn shares interest and share profit when the China shareholder can make decision to sell himself/herself shares in the the high price, then he/she can earn money when he/she can sell the China company's shares in the high sale share price position.

If China has many Chinese like to spend time to carry on investing shares activities. Themselves shares buying and selling behaviors will influence China has many companies can increase fund from many Chinese shareholders in order to have enough money to expand or develop themselves businesses in China in long term.

Consequently, when China can have many Chinese like to attempt to carry on buying and selling shares investing behaviors in China share market. Themselves buying and selling shares behaviors can help many Chinese companies have effort to increase enough money or capital in order to continue to do their businesses in long term absolutely. So, it explains why when many Chinese become shareholders , they can assist China will have many companies continue to develop their businesses if many Chinese like to carry on shares buying and selling investing behaviors in long time in China financial investment market nowadays in behavioral economic view.

Why has any individual country have many people invest share behavior which can influence the country's macro consumption desire?
I shall apply shares market buying and selling investment behavior to explaiin why shares investment behavior which may impact the country's overal consumption desire as below:
In behavioral economic view, I assume that when the coutry has many people have interest to attempt to carry on shares buying and selling investment behavior, then their frequent shares buying and selling behaviors which may bring negactive consumption desire or shopping desire of these shares investors their consumer behavior.
The reason is simple, when the country has many share buyers number suddenly been increasing rapidly. Consequently, these large group share investors must need to spend much time to research any kinds of company shares variations, whether when their share prices will rise up of fall down in order to achieve buying the company's shares in the lowest price and selling the company's shares in the highest price level in order to earn profit.
Basic on this reason, they must need to spend much extra time to research share prices changing behavior every day, e.g. one working person will wait to leave his/her job, after he/she can spend time to gather data to research the day's share price changing behavior after dinner. So, the working person's right time may be his/her share price market research behavior. Before he/she may spend his/her night time to go to shopping after dinner, but nowadays, he/she will fogive to do his/her shopping behavior before dinner or after dinner at hight sometime. He/she will make decision to spend much night time to turn on computer to click on share market website to research his/her share purchase choice to investigate whether his/her share price whether it rises up or falls down at the moment in order to make his/her share buying or selling decision at ever night time.
I mean the when the country has many people are share investors, their shares investment behavioral spenging time which will influence many shops lose customers at might often because the country will have many people feel need to spend night time to turn on computer or watch television to investigate share price variation. So, the country will have many people / share investors choose to stay at home in order to carry on share price variation investigation behavior, they need to listen share market update news from radios or watch the share market update news from computer or TV at home every night. Consequenly, they must reduce

times to leave themselves homes at night. So, their shopping behavior also will be reduced. Because these share investors feel need to spend time to investigate share price variation news at homes which can bring economic benefits (high opportunity benefits) when they choose to forgive to leave homes to go to shopping times (opportunity cost) every night.

On conclusion, it seems that when the country has many people are share investors, then their share price investigating behavior may bring negative shopping emotion at night. Consequently, the country's any one shop may lose many customers from this share investor consumer group in behavioral economic view. Hence, when the country's share investors number had been increasing rapidly, it will influence any shops lose many customers from this share investing customer group at night frequenly in short time, even long time in behavioral economic view, because their shopping desires or shopping emotion will be brought negative feeling when they make decisions to spend much time to listen radios or watch TV or computers share price update nes at night. Hence, share market will bring negative impact to influence consumer shopping desire or negative shopping emotion in behavioral economic view.

Can technology influence human shopping behavioral change?

Nowadays, technological development has reached mature stage, whether technological mature stage may bring positive or negative shopping emotion influence to global consumers. I shall aplly internet inventin or ecommerce shopping channel tool to explain whether internet technology can bring postive or negative influence to global consumer behavior in behavioral economic view.

Internet is a good technological tool, it brings e-commerce business chance. In fact, commonly, global has have many businessmen choose to use internet channel to carry on their products transactions between global online-buyers and their electronic websites. So, global many shoppers had begun to feel online shopping is more convenient to compare visiting shops shopping. Their shopping behaviors have been changed from internet technological tool. Global has many shoppers choose to buy any products from any overseas or local businessmen their web stores. They only need to spend time to find any businessmen their webstores to choose the most suitable products to pay visa to buy from their webstores. at homes. So, in general, global had have may shoppers had changed their shopping behaviors from visiting shops to visiting webstores at homes often.

So, it seems that internet technological tool had influenced global many shops disappear, but internet webstores will be replaced their actual shops on streets. Some of businessmen either they choose webstores to replace shops or choose websotes and shops both or still keep shops only. Hence, internet tool influences global businessmen have three kinds of products sale channels to let globa local and overseas consumers to choose how to buy their products.

However, in fact, many of global shoppers, youngers and olders had begun to accept to buy any products from webstores. They feel to spend time to leave homes to visit shops , their shopping behaviors will be wasted time to not essential part to their daily lives. Hence, since internet technological invention, it had changed many consumers their traditional visiting shops shopping habit to change to buying products from webstores channel.

However, on the one hand, internet creates webstores ecommerce shopping channel to let global many consumers do not need to leave homes to go to shopping. It brings negative visiting shops shopping emotion to global general consumers nowadays. But on the other hand, it also brings positive visiting internet webstores shopping emotion to global general consumer nowadays. So, it seems that global many consumers feel that they often do not need to spend much time to go out shopping. Many global consumers feel convenient and enjoy to choose any products to buy from different internet webstores, when the online buyer chooses the most suitable product, he she only needs to pay visa card to buy the product from the online seller's webstore conveniently at home.

Hence, online shopping can bring economic benefit to online buyers, e.g. avoiding walking time or spending transport fare to visit the shop to go to shopping, shortening or reducing shopping time to do another important matter.

On conclusion, global many consumers began feel online shopping can bring more economic benefits on shortening shopping time, avoiding transport fare spending aspect. So, online shopping will be popular shopping behavior for future long time. It may encourage global many shoppers can make rapid shopping decision in short time in order to carry on any products buying transaction to global any one online shopper in short time easily in behavioral economic view. So, global many businessmen had begun to build themselves one attraction webstore in order to persuade different countries consumers to choose to click themselves webstores from internet channel to buy any kinds of products in short time easily.

So, internet technology had changed consumers traditional shopping behaviors to build positive online shopping emotion as well as raise online sellers' any products sale chance easily in behavioral economic view.

Why and how human behavior may influence the country's economic growth or recession?

When one country has many people choose to do the same matter for one period, whether their behavior may influence the country's pvera; economic growth or recession . I shall attempt to indicate cases toexplain their relationship as below:

For flowing rubblish behavioral case example, do you feel that when the country has many people often flow rubblish on the streets, instead of their flowing rubblish behavior may bring streets dirty? But, their flowing rubblish behavior may explain that this country has people may have enough money to buy food to ear, or enough cloths to wear, enough bottles of water to drink, even they may have enough money to buy new television, radio, refrigeraters , washing machines, desktops or laptops electronic home products from old to new to use in order to satisfy their living needs. So, when they flow old electronic home products, their flowing old home electronic products behaviors may seem that they have enough money to buy other new home electronic products to replace old home electronic products to use at homes.

However, it seems thaat this country ought have many people have jobs to do. So, many of them, they can easy to make purchase decison to flow any old home electronic products and buy any new home electronic products to use . Because this country has many people have jobs to do. So, they can often not use old home electonic products to become rubblishs to flow on streets after they had bought any kinds of new home electronic homes.

In fact, it also implies that this country's economy grows rapidly. So, many businesses can glow up rapdly. When they expanded their businesses, they must need to increase employees number in order to let they help themselves to raise productivity or serve their clients absolutely. So, when the country has many businesses can grow up, it seems that its economy must be better or it is improved to compare past. Due to many different kinds of home electronic products had been often bought to use by this country people in this period. So, this country's any streets can be observed that expensive electronic home products were flowed on streets anywhere. then, this country will have many electronic home products sellers can sell their home electronic products very easily. When this country has many people can find any kinds of jobs to do easily. So, due to unemploymen rate had been decreasing.

In behavioral economic view, as this many electronic home products rubblish country case, we can observe this country may have many people have jobs to do. So, consumption number has been increased long time. So, cheap food, or expensive home electronic products may be rubblish on any streets. This country's people , their flowing rubblish behaviors may be explained that many of people have enough jobs to do, so they have ability to buy any good taste food to eat or buy any kinds of expensive electronic home products to use. So, this country's economy may be improved for this long period. So, in behavioral economic view, when this country can have many electronic home products rubblishs are flowed on anywherer in streets frequently. It seems that this country will have many people have jobs to do, so it causes they often change old home electronic products or replaced them easily, when they have enough income to spend to buy any kinds of new home electronic products to use at homes easily. Moreover, their flowing old electronic home products behaviors also indicate that this country has many people their salaries may be increased in possible from their emplyers. When this country can have many different kinds of home electornic products are sold. It means that this country's electronic home products needs or demand had been increasing, due to many people have jobs to do and income increases to excite their living of needs also improve. Consequently, this country may seem have better economic improvement. We can observe from this country's electronic home products rubblish increasing income in theis period.

On conclusion, this country ought experience economic growth at this period. So, " flowing expensive electronic home rubblish increasing number " may seem that this country's economic growth is rapidly in this period, due to many people have jobs to do as well as salaries increase in this period.

Technology how impacts human behavior changing?

Technology how influences human behavior to bring changing? For example, online share purchase and sale transaction from smart phone brings share investor can do share buying or selling transation in any where and any time conveniently, non manual driving auto vehicle, bring car owner feels comfortable and spends free time to do other matter, e.g. reading, listening mucis in himself or herself car freely. electrical energy vehicle can help car owner to reduce air polluton and it can brings the drivers do not feel drive long time in any journeys in order to avoid air pollution for environmental protection responsible car drivers in our societies. Thus, they will drive long time in any journeys when they can drive electronic energy cars to replace oil energy cars.

However, online technology can also bring consumers can choose to stay at homes to buy any things from seller individual online webstore conveniently. Such as online technology can bring shoppers do not need to spend much time to visit shops to buy any things. They can choose any kinds of products from any online sellers individual online webstores conveniently at homes. Online technology excite busy consumers can make purchase decision easily as well as it can help online sellers sell any kinds of products from internet easily.

In behavioral economic view, technology can change human behavior to be improved, it can let human feels comfortable, more free time ro use, rapid making any decisions, such as apply smart phones to make share purchase or sale transaction decision, online shopping decision, even travelling any where decision in short time, when the traveller finds the most cheap hotel accommodation room price and air ticket price frm any travel agent online tourism webstore, then the potential travel customer can follow the online hotel accommodation price and air ticket price data to make decision when to buy the air ticket from the airline travel agent or make decision when to prebook which hotel accommodation room to go to the country to travel from online travel agent tourism webstores. So, technology can encourage global any country travelers to make anywhere to trvel rapidly. If the traveler can find the country's general hotel rooms and airline tickets prices had been decreasing more sightly. The traveler may make travel decision to choose the country to travel in short time, then he/she can prebook the country;s any hotel room and airline ticket to pay by visa fraom the country's any hotel and airline travel agent webstores., before one week, even one month or more easily. Hence, online technology can also encourage traveler individual frequent travel times to be increased, due to global travelers can find any hotel rooms and airline tickets prices from internet conveniently at homes. They do not need to spend time to visit any airline travel agent to enquire travel choice country's hotel rooms prices and airline ticket prices. They can compare global travel of countries choices ' all hotels rooms and airline agents air tickets prices to make prebook airline seat and hotel room decision before one week, one month even six months early.

On conclusion, online technology can encourage global travelers can make travelling any where and when traveling time desicions easily. It can excite tourism industry develops in long time. Also, such as electricity cars invention can encourage environment protection car owners do car purchase decision easily, because they can choose to drive electronic energy cars to replace oil energy cars in order to avoid air pollution occurs easily. So, electronic cars can increase electronic car purchasrs number, due to many of environmental protection attitude of car owners can choose to drive electricity cars to bring air cleans, even non -manual driving cars can encourage lazy driving and free time driving car owners to choose to buy non-manual (artificial intelligent) cars to drive , because they can spend much free time to read, listen music or do any matters in themselves cars, they do not need to drive cars, robotic (AI) auto driving machine is such one non-manual driver to help them to drive themselves cars confidently. So, non-manual driving cars can attract lazy and enjoying free time driving car owners to choose to buy to replace traditional manual cars to drive easily. Moreover, online share transaction can help any share investors to make share buying and selling decision in short time easily. When they can apply smart phones technological tool to carry on share buying and selling activities easily. They can observe any share rising or falling price suitation from smart phones in any where any any time easily. So, smart phone technology can help global any shareholders to make share purchase and sale transaction easily. So, technology can encourage human makes decision in short time rapidly.

How and why employees behaviors may influence economy development?

In behavioral economy view,I believe the country's any organizational employees behavior may bring indirect relationship to influence the country's long term economic development. I shall indicate past manufacture industry social development period to explain their relationship. For many countries' past business activities had belonged to manufacturing industry, such as US, UK past before 1980 year, it focused on steel manufacturing and steel manufacturing related machine products. So, US, Uk developed countries manufacturing industries may be past main country's economic income sources. I assume US , UK past had one million number different kinds of industries. They ought had about seven houndred thousand number organizational businesses were belonged to manufactured industry. They may include:

Steel manufacturing and steel related machine manufacturing, e.g. vehicle manufacturing, home appliances, e.g. washing machine, television, radio, refrigerate cooler, heater, air condition etc. different kinds of different kinds of steel -related manufacturing machine, they were manufactured from US, UK steel machine manufacturers. So, US, Uk the other three hundred thousand number industry may be general service industry, e.g. hotel service, restaurent, cinema, public transport service, tourism lesiure , wine bar, supermarket etc. different kinds of non-manufacturing industries business organizations were operated in UK, US past before 1980 year.

So, in UK, US developed countries industry development history, they ought have high percentage of businesses belonged to steel related manufacturing machine and steel products. Also, in the past before 1980 year, US, Uk business employers , they employed many workers are manufacturing workers. They needed to spend long time to work in factories. They were skillful workers, and they are trained to manufacturing cars, washing machine, television, heater, etc. even steel itself different kinds of steel related products to prepare to deliver to their shops to sell to US, Uk local or overseas clients.

So, I believe that past UK, US ought employ many employees, they belonged to skillful manufacturing workers, manufacture increasing steel machine or steel related machine number of products rapidly daily. So, if UK, US had had many of these manufacturing factories owned high skillful workers, then their manufacturing steel-related machine or steel both kinds of products number must be influenced to raise rapidly. Consequently, their steel machine manufacturing products would been exported to overseas or would been sold to local both markets , they may be influenced to raise sale number. They (these manufacturing workers) needed to be trained to know how to manufactur these different kinds of machine products in the efficient teams and they ought to be trained to raise their efficiencies in order to shorten time to manufacturing many kinds of steel related manufacturing machine or steel itself products rapidly. So , if their efficiencies and manufacturing performance was improved, these US, UK any one manufacturing worker and their teams ought achieve raising productivities significantly.

Hence, when past UK, US manufacturing industry development period, if these two countries‘ any manufacturing factories could have many manufacturing workers could be trained to be skillful and proficient manufacturing workers. Then, in past every day to these factories workers, they ought help their steel or steel related manufacturing employers to raise any kinds of machine or steel products number in every team. So, when past in the manufacturing industry development, US, UK could have many factories' manufacturing workers themselves steel or steel related machine products manufacturing skill could be trained to to improve to any kinds of these machine or steel manufacuring products quality as well as their products number could be influenced to raise by themselves skillful improvement significantly every day.

Then, what would be influenced to occur to past UK, US manufacturing industry period? In behavioral economic view, when these two manufacturing industry developed countries, such as UK, US , if they had many factories workers can be trained to improve their skill in order to achieve any kinds of steel or steel-related machine products quality could be improved as well as products manufacturing number could be also increased absolutely.

In consequence, past UK and US both countries ought increase themselves any kinds of steel and steel related machine products number to be supplied to themselves local shops to let local clients to choose any one kind of machine manufacturing products to buy easily as well as they could also export to supply overseas any countries to buy their different kinds of steel or steel related machine products to let overseas steel or steel related manufacturing machine product buyers, they can have many of these different kinds of these steel or steel-related different kinds of manufacturing machine from UK and UK these both countries easily to compare other countries.

On conclusion, I believe that past US, and UK macro manufacturing industry income GDP would increase significantly. So, they would have good economic growth performance because when many of these manufacturing workers themselves manufacturing effort could be improved. So, it explained when employees manufacturing abilities can influence economic growth indirectly.

Robots invention whether they can help organizations to raise efficiencies or inefficiencies?

In behavioral economic view, in any organizations, when the organization hopes its worker teams can raise efficiencies , the organization may choose to increase more workers number and/or it can provide training to improve these workets themselves skills in order to raise their efficiencies. For one warehouse example, when the warehouse increases many goods , they are needed to delivered these goods from the shelves to the delivering destination locations. If this warehouse supervisors feel these workers themselves goods delivery speeds are slow, which is possible due to this warehouse's workers number is not enough. So, this warehouse supervisor ought increase workers number in order to increase their goods delivery speed in order to deliver goods from the shelves to every indicated goods delivery destination in order to let any one lorry driver can transport the right kinds of goods and ensure the accurate goods number to transport to any one client home rapidly.

However, if this warehouse supervisor planed to buy several warehouse goods delivery robots to assist these warehouse workers to find the right kinds of goods from shelves and then deliver to the right destination location in the warehouse. So, these warehouse orkers can concentrate on counting the accurate goods number and ensuring the right kinds of goods in order to prepare to let lorry drivers to transport these goods to these goods of buyers themselvers homes rapidly. Consequently, in the first step, robots can concentrate on finding th right goods from shelves and delivers them to the right goods transportation of location destination. Then, in the second step, these warehouse workers can concentrate on counting the accurate goods number and ensuring the right kinds of goods in order to prepare to put them to the lorry. Consequently, when warehouse robots and warehouse workers can cooperate to work together, the most important, robots, can deal on finding the right kinds of goods and deal on delivering the accurate number of goods of job duty as well as these warehouse workers can only concentrte on counting the right kinds of goods number in order to avoid it has none any mistake of wrong kinds of goods and inaccurate goods of delivery number to be transported to the lorry and to deliver to any one buyer's home.

So, it seems that warehouse robots ought help any one warehouse worker to raise himself efficiency and avoid goods delivery of mistake occurrence easily as well as their help to warehouse workers that can let any one goods buyer feels their goods can be delivered to their homes rapidly. Moreover, warehouse robots can also help these warehouse workers to raise efficiencies because warehouse robots can help them to shorten goods delivery time between any one shelf and any one goods delivery destination of location in the warehuse because robots may help them to find the right kinds of goods from the right shelf in the short time. So, any one worker does not need to spend long time to seek anywhere is the right shelf location

for the kind of goods when the kind of goods are needed to deliver to the buyer's home from lorry. Warehouse robots can help them to do this aspect of " finding the goods from the right shelf in short time job duty". So, any one warehouse worker only needed tospend less time to do the counting of any right kind of goods number and ensuring the right kind of goods job duty. Consequently, this warehouse 's any one worker, his any one kind of goods delivery time may be reduced, because robots' assistance and they may have more confidence to avoid mistake to deliver the wrong number of goods and/or the wrong kind of goods to any one goods buyer's home.
On conclusion, it seems that warehouse robots ought may help any one warehouse worker to raise efficiency for any one team in the warehouse as well as the warehouse any one supervisor does not need to spend much time to observe any one worker individual performance for " goods delivery job duty aspect" because their goods delivery job duty that had been replaced to do by these several warehouse robots. Robots can achieve the more accurate of right kinds of goods and the right number of goods delviery job performance to compare any one of human warehouse worker themselves right kinds of goods of delivery and right number of goods of delivery job performance. So, when robots can participate to cooperate with this warehouse's any one worker to do their goods of delivery job duty in this warehouse every day. Then, robots can raies any one of supervisor individual confidence in order to let they do not need to spend time to observe any one of worker individual whose goods of delivery job performane. They can concentrate on supervising any one worker whose goods transport to lorry in the final step in order to avoid to deliver wrong goods number and / or wrong kind of goods to any one goods buyer's home every day. Consequently, this warehouse's overall teams of their delviery of goods performance many be improved by robotss' participatin to goods of delivery task as well as this warehouse's oveall teams themselves efficiencies may be influenced to raise by robots' goods of delivery task participation.

Why social behavior may influence organizational strategy needs to be changed ?
Why any organizations need to know whether nowadays social behaivor how has been changing in order to implement the kind of the most right strategy to achieve the profit aim pursue in possible. I shall indicate nowadays ecommerce or online, customer shopping behavior to explain

above question concerns they ought have close relationship between social behavior and organizational strategic choice or organizational behavioral changing need.

On nowadays ecommerce business, or online shopping model, this kind of shopping model in global many young and old age consumers like to apply internet tool to choose any country sellers website stores in order to stay at home to buy any kinds of products from themselves webstores in global societies.

In fact, online shopping model had been popular for long time above to twenty years. Most of global sellers will make decision to design themselves webstores in order to attract global many online buyers to choose to buy their products from themselves webstores. So, it seems that social consumers purchase behaviors had been changed to online shopping from internet invention.

Hence, social consumers purchase behavioral changes may influence any organizations' strategies need to be changed from visiting shops purchase strategy model to online purchase strategy model, if the seller still concentrate on concentrate on considerate how to design itelf , but neglects to considerate how to design itself webstore, e.g. how to design attract product photos to put on itself webstore, how to arrange sale price information location to be putted on webstore and visa card payment location on itself webstore in order to let any one online buyer can feel very easier to buy itself any kinds of products from itself webstore. Then, its potential online buyers will be influenced to increase number when they can find this online seller itself any kinds of products photes and every kinds of product sale price information and visa card payment channel locations easily from itself webstore.

So, it implies that nowadays any one seller ought need to design one webstore to let any one online overseas and domestic consumers can have chance to click itself webstore to choose any one kind of product to buy conveniently when he/she does not hope to leave him/her home to go to shop, because nowadays social shopping behaviors had been influenced to change when internet invention, them it gives another online purchase method to replace visiting shops purchase method to global any one buyer in nowadays societies.

So, if nowadays any one seller still concentrate on how to design itself shop display in order to put any kinds of product on shelf in order to let any one visiting shop customer to find the kind of product to buy, but it neglects to change to choose to pursue another new technological shopping method, such as webstore purchase method in order to implement effective strategy to design the most right webstore as well as in order to attract global overseas and local consumers to find itself webstore easily from website and find its any one kind of product phots and sale price and visa card payment button in order to choose to buy itself any kinds of products in the short time. Consequently I believe that the seller will lose many customers from overseas and local when its other same or similar product sellers choose to design themselves webstores in order to let global any one product buyer can buy themselves any one kind of product when they can pay visa card to buy their products from them webstores conveniently when they stay at home habitly. Then, the seller will lose many global potential customers in long time.

On conclusion, in behavioral economic view, any consumer behavioral social changing, which will influence any in order to avoid customers number loses significantly . In future time, organizations need to make rapid decision in order to implement the most reasonable and the most useful strategy in order to avoid global potential customers number reduces or lose them in long time. So, social behavioral changing environment ought influence any global organizations need to decide how to change themselves strategies in order to avoid customers loses significantly in future time.

How and why human behavior may influence economic growth or recession?

May ourselves daily behaviors influence our global societial continue economic growth or recession? Do they have cause and effect close relationship between human behaviors and global economic growth or recession? I shall apply behavioral economic theory to analyze and explain whether ourselves daily behaviors and our global societial economic growth or recession which have close cause and effect relationship as below:

Every country itself economic development must depend on any business activities, otherwise, any kinds of business activities must need ourselves business activities or behaviors in order to achieve any business activities as well as achieve the country's overall economic development in macro view. However, any country's overall business activites or behaviors which must depend on any kinds of individual businessmen, themselves employees daily working behavior or activity or performance in order to help them to attract or increase many clients number to acieve " earning profit" aim.

So, it seems that any individual business, itself overall every department individual working behavior is one main factor to influence the company's overall business performance.

For agricultural fruit and meat food farming industry example, such as New Zealand is a farming main target industry country. It had had many New Zealanders were daily themselves own farming businesses for many years. Their farming businesses include growing fruit, sheep, cow, pig pork, meat etc. food sale business. If the New Zealand farmer owned a large size farming land, then he will choose either growing fruit or feeding sheeps, pigs, cows to be meat to to transport to New Zealand supermarkets to help them to sell to their farmers meet to New Zealanders in order to earn profit. Thus, if the New Zealand farmer owned large size of farming lands, then he needs to employ many farming employees (farming workers) to help him to carry on farming business daily tasks, e.g. picking up friuts, feeding pigs, cows, sheeps to eat food daily. These daily farming jobs are very important to influence this New Zealand farmer's meats or fruits sale number whether they can be easy or diffcult to sell in New Zealand supermarkets , if these farming workers can own encough farming knowledge or skill to know how to pick up fruits method and make judgement to know whether it is right time to pick up the kind of fruits from the trees , as well as know how feed this pigs, sheeps, cows to eat food in order to let they are better health. Consequently, their farming behaviors which can let these animals can provide the best taste and enough meat from these animals to let New Zealander to buy to eat from New Zealand any one supermarket. Even these New Zealand farming workers can know whether the kinds of fruits, e.g. oranges, apples, gapes etc. fruits whether they ought be picked up from the trees at the right time. Consequently, they can make judgement to decide to pick up any kinds of the best taste fruits to let any one New Zealander to buy to eat from any one supermarket in New Zealand. Otherwise, if they do not make judegement to know whether the kind of fruit ought not be picked up because they still need longer time to continue grow up to increase fruit size and better taste from the trees in order to let any one fruit buyer can feel better taste when they eat this kind of fruit later. If they can buy this kind of fruit to eat later, then this New Zealand farmer's his fruit buyers can buy the best taste of this kind of fruit to eat from an yone supermarket in New Zealand. Consequently, many New Zealand supermarkets will choose to buy any kinds of fruits from this farmer fruit supplier when they feel this farmer's fruits can provide more better taste fruits to compare other

farmers' fruits.
Thus, due to New Zealand is one farming main income source country. It's any kinds of fruits and meats need to be export to overseas to sell , instead of local sale. It's GDP percent is very high to whole country 's overall income source. So, any one New Zealand farmer individual and any one farming worker individual working behavior will influence its economy whether it is influenced to grow or recession possible. Moreover, it also seems that farming workers' farming knowledge and skill will influence themselves farming daily activities to achieve the aim of the number of increase or decrease to any kinds of fruits whether they are better taste or the number of increase of decrease to any kinds of meats whether they are better taste to supply to any one New Zealand fruit or meat buyers to eat from any one New Zealand supermarket. So, it implies that any one New Zealand farming worker individual farming behavior may influence any kinds of fruits or any kinds of meat taste because they are transported to any one supermarket to sell in New Zealand.
Consequently, if New Zealans had many farmers can teach god farming knowledge and skill to let their any one farming workers know how to decide judgement to decide when it is right time to pick up any kinds of fruits from trees , or how to grow them on soil in order to let they can grow rapidly. Then, many different kinds of fruits can be provided to let any one New Zealanders can eat the best taste of fruits when their fruits are supplied to any one New Zealand supermarkets. Even, if they knew how to feed foods to pigs, cows, sheeps to eat daily. Then they can be more health and they can provide the best taste of meats to let any one New Zealanders can buy their meats from any one New Zealand supermarkets. Moreover, their fruits and meats can be transported to overseas to let any one country fruits or meats buyers can choose any kinds of New Zealand meats and fruits to buy to eat from themselves countries supermarkets. Then, many overseas fruit and meat buyers will perfer to choose New Zealand any kinds of fruits or meats to buy to compare other countries fruits or meats to buy when they go to any one local supermarkets.
On conclusion, it seems that New Zealand farming workers themselves farming behavior may influence their farming employers any kinds of fruits or meats sale number and income because their farming task behaviors must influence whether their fruits or meats taste are the better taste or worse taste to compare their other local farmers (the farmer competitors) whose fruits or meats taste. If tthe farmer's any one farming worker can be

trained to learn how to know to feed animals skill and when is the most right time to pick up any kinds of fruits from trees or how to grow them on the soil methods. Due to these farming worker individual farming behavior may influence his different finds of fruits and meats sale number to be increase or decrease, so these any one New Zealand farmer must need to depend on any one farming worker whose farming working methods, if their farming working behaviors can be the best to influence any kinds of fruits to grow rapid or any kinds of pigs, cows, sheeps animals grow up rapidly , then their sale number may be increase significantly and their taste can be improved to let any New Zealand or overseas meat or fruit buyer to buy to eat to feel from any one New Zealand or overseas supermarkets, then New Zealand's agriculture industry must be influenced to increase. In the world, any one fruit or meat buyer must choose to buy New Zealand's fruit and meat to eat in prefer to compare other countries' fruits and meats. So, New Zealand's GDP may be influenced to raise from any one New Zealand farming worker individual farming working behaviors.

www.ingramcontent.com/pod-product-compliance
Ingram Content Group UK Ltd.
Pitfield, Milton Keynes, MK11 3LW, UK
UKHW041638190726
13854UKWH00006B/2569